Cybersecurity

Cybersecurity

Everything You, Your Family, And Every
Small Business Owner Needs to Know

Phillip J. Ferraro

PJF Publishing

Published by PJF Publishing
Tampa, Florida

Cybersecurity / Phillip J. Ferraro — first edition

Edited by Peter Letzelter.

Library of Congress Number: 2025908097
Paperback ISBN: 979-8-9929396-0-6
eBook ISBN: 979-8-9929396-1-3

PRAISE FOR CYBERSECURITY

"This book is an essential guide for anyone who wants to feel confident and secure in today's digital world. It's clear, practical, and filled with real solutions that both individuals and business owners can apply immediately. Whether you're just beginning to understand cybersecurity or you're already tech-aware, this book will open your eyes to risks you didn't know you were taking—and empower you with the knowledge to protect yourself and those you care about. I highly recommend it."
—*Dr. Peggy McColl, New York Times Best-Selling Author and Trusted Mentor to High Achievers Worldwide*

"When it comes to cybersecurity, Phil is the expert. *Cybersecurity: Everything an Individual, Family, or Business Needs to Know* is a must read for all. Phil takes his years of experience in a wide variety of cyber roles and encapsulates the critical lessons he's learned into a well-considered, easy-to-understand approach. Even the most seasoned security professionals should read it."
—*Malcolm Harkins, Global CISO, Chief Security, and*

Trust Officer

"Phil's no-nonsense guide to cybersecurity is brought to life with alarming, but real, scenarios that have had far-reaching effects. Phil delivers a refreshing and powerful approach to educate individuals and businesses alike, without the typical scare tactics surrounding cybersecurity. Readers will greatly benefit from the perspective of this passionate, world-class Global Chief Information Security Officer to quickly learn how to best protect themselves from ever-changing cyber threats."
—*Mike Stango, Executive Director, Security 50*

"As one of the nation's top cybersecurity leaders—trusted by Fortune 500 companies and Congressional committees alike—Phillip Ferraro brings unmatched authority and real-world insight to today's digital dangers. This book is a vital, urgent resource for families, small businesses, and anyone looking to take control of their cybersecurity. With Ferraro as your guide, you're not just prepared—you're empowered."
—*Chris Ancharski, Global Cybersecurity Community Builder and Startup Advisor*

Dedicated to my wife, Sandra Ferraro. Thank you for always being there for me, and for all your unconditional love, encouragement, and support.

Thank you for understanding those many years of extremely long days and nights and travel around the world on my cybersecurity missions.

Thank you for listening to many, many Zoom and other video calls solving people's cybersecurity issues and concerns.

Without you, I would not be where I am.

CONTENTS

INTRODUCTION

Dear Reader,

There was once a time when a business's worst nightmare would be a group of clandestine and hooded thieves smashing a window, cracking the safe or cash register, and making away with a pile of hard-earned cash. But times change.

Today's threat landscape is significantly different, as well as much more sophisticated, aggressive—and scarier than ever. A well-trained, computer-savvy thief can enter a home or business while you're working or watching TV and extract extremely sensitive and protected data. With the click of a few buttons, they can open the floodgates and obtain personally identifiable information (PII), or in the case of business's client information, credit card numbers, intellectual property, trade secrets, and other content that could cost a company time, effort, and endless amounts of money. Masked bandits have been replaced by calculating and infiltrating computer hackers. These are the cybersecurity thieves.

Cybercriminals do not care who they steal the money from—businesses, individuals, or family members. Identity theft is one of the world's fastest-growing forms of cybercrime today and has more than tripled over the last decade. In 2024, the Federal Trade Commission stated that nearly 1.4 million cases of identity theft, out of a total of 5.7 million fraud and identity theft reports, have been reported across the United States. Credit card fraud has long been one of the most common forms of identity theft, but a new fast-growing crime—synthetic identity theft—is now occurring. Cybercriminals use your stolen social security number but attach it to a different name and address—though the credit issues still get tied back to you.

For businesses, a cybersecurity breach can put small to midsize organizations out of business or, at the very least, inflict damage that could reach into the hundreds of thousands of dollars. That may pale in comparison to the significant damage to a brand's reputation.

Business leaders are responsible for not only the traditional success of a company but cybersecurity issues as well. They can be held fiscally accountable for a cyber breach. As such, they should anticipate and prepare for future events that could significantly impact their organization. One of those events is a cybersecurity breach. Leaders of companies face enormous cyber challenges: a limited understanding of cybersecurity business risks, responsibility for the full financial and business impact of a breach, and analyzing and evaluating the investments necessary to protect against these threats.

The goal of this book is to provide an in-depth understanding of these significant issues while learning exactly what steps you—whether an individual, family member, or business leader—can take to properly prepare for today's constantly evolving threat landscape.

My name is Phillip Ferraro and I'm one of the top Chief Information Security Officers (CISO) in the country. For more than 25 years, I've defended organizations against the world's most sophisticated cyberattackers. I give international keynote talks on all aspects of cybersecurity and am one of the few CISOs to make presentations on cybersecurity and advanced threats to Senate and Congressional committees on Capitol Hill.

In short, I have seen it all.

The last several years of my career have been specifically focused on helping individuals, families, and small businesses better protect themselves.

Most books on cybersecurity focus either on defensive technologies or a very speculative high-level approach. The problem is that the tech approach is written for CISOs and the staff who implement such technologies. This high-level approach delivers a 50,000-foot overview, describing threats and couching them in the language of fear, uncertainty, and doubt. Such books do not take the time to provide the details necessary to understand the overall concepts and sensitivities found within the cybersecurity realm—how threats can impact an organization and what can be done to ensure you, your family, and your business are safeguarded.

This book provides hands-on tips and procedures that can be implemented right now. Because I have many years of experience presenting to and advising boards of directors and C-suite executives, I provide an in-the-trenches approach to handling cybersecurity issues before they occur. I provide clear and concise facts about cybersecurity and how to develop comprehensive defenses—not only for a business but for families as well. This book will help readers immediately apply this knowledge. Comprehensive cyber programs include many functional areas; this book cuts through the fog to provide a clear picture of where and what to focus on to effectively manage cyber risk.

I am confident that reading this book will be an excellent investment of time and money and that you will keep it close and refer to it often as a reference book. You'll also learn a great deal about the cybersecurity industry, including how some of the best-known information breaches that have occurred. There are valuable lessons from these stories, including a much better understanding of cybersecurity threats, why big companies are getting breached, and what to do to significantly lower risk, raise security, and avoid becoming a victim. I cover how to implement a comprehensive cybersecurity program and get it up and running immediately, the full impact and financial effects of a potential breach, and the steps necessary to manage a cybersecurity crisis.

We now live in a world with cyber threats around every corner. One small data breach can be catastrophic to a business or family. But preventative maintenance is not nearly as difficult as you might think. Investing a little bit of time and money now can be the difference between success and demise. So, together, we can overcome the new generation of thieves who can literally rob you blind.

After reading this book and you would like personalized assistance, please reach out. I am very happy to provide cybersecurity consultations and can be reached through my website at phillipferraro.com.

PART 1

PROTECTING
YOURSELF AND
YOUR FAMILY

CHAPTER 1

Are You at Risk?

I have seen so many cyberattacks. And not just on big corporations. Cybercriminals really do not care about the size of a business or how much money is in a bank account. They just want to steal information or money in any way they can. And they love to go after the easy targets.

That's what this book is all about—making you a hard target and making the cybercriminals go somewhere else. Cyberattacks are becoming increasingly common, targeting not just businesses but also individuals and families. These attacks can range from identity theft to ransomware, phishing, and other forms of malicious activity.

In 2024, the risk of cyberattacks on individuals and families remains a significant concern. The cyber threat landscape is complex and constantly evolving, which makes it important to stay informed and prepared.

Common vulnerabilities include limited awareness of current types of phishing attacks, weak passwords, not using two-factor authentication, unsecured Wi-Fi networks, mobile devices set up improperly, the use of outdated software, and more.

Who are Cybercriminals?

I like to talk about who cybercriminals are. Many years ago, I read the book The Art of War, written by the Chinese general, strategist, and philosopher Sun Tzu 2,500 years ago (I'm old but not quite that old). This book is so good it's still in print today. One of my favorite quotes is, "Know your enemy and know yourself; in a hundred battles, you will never be defeated." That is still so true today, 2,500 years later—especially in terms of cyber warfare.

Cybercriminals can be individuals, an organized group, or even an operation supported by nation-states. They can function locally or internationally. Their motivations vary from financial gain to political agendas, espionage, or simply causing disruption.

A study from the University of Maryland's A. James Clark School of Engineering reveals that cyberattacks occur at an alarming rate of over 2,200 times daily, with someone falling victim every 39 seconds.

According to the World Economic Forum (WEF), if cybercrime were a country, it would be the world's third-largest global economy after only the United States and China. Cybersecurity Ventures, an industry think tank, projects that its impact will reach $10.5 trillion by 2025.

Let's look at each of the three main categories of cybercriminals:

HACTIVISTS

At one end of the spectrum are hacktivists. These are very, very skilled hackers who do it for ideological reasons. Maybe they just don't like the color of your logo—or they are acting for political reasons or to expose perceived injustices. They hack in and steal very sensitive information, then threaten to expose it on the internet if you don't change whatever it is they do not like. Most hacktivist attacks occur on businesses and government organizations.

For example, one notable hacktivist cyberattack was an assault by the group Anonymous on the Church of Scientology in 2008. Known as Project Chanology, it was initiated in response to attempts to remove a video featuring Tom Cruise discussing Scientology on the internet. The group launched a series of actions using various hacking techniques, including distributed denial-of-service (DDoS) attacks that overwhelmed Scientology websites, making them inaccessible. They also organized real-world protests—including information warfare, public demonstrations, and other online protests—by utilizing various digital media to spread their message against what they perceived as the church's censorship.

This incident is notable not just for its scale and impact but also because it marked a significant use of cyberattacks for ideological rather than financial reasons. It brought attention to the concept of hacktivism as a form of protest and demonstrated how cyberattacks could be used as tools for political and social activism.

NATION-STATES

On the other end of the spectrum, nation-states carry out state-sponsored cyberterrorism. While this is primarily countries attacking other countries for political or military intelligence, going after critical infrastructure—financial services, energy, oil, gas, transportation, and communications—also occurs. Additionally, intellectual property (IP) is also a target. If IP is stolen, then state-supported businesses can go to market faster and cheaper and not have to spend large sums of money on research and development.

Several US companies have been driven out of business after their intellectual property was stolen and the responsible nation-state provided it to one of its companies.

Here are some notable cases of cyberattacks by nation-states that have caused significant damage:

SolarWinds. In December 2020, the IT firm Solar-Winds was compromised by a nation-state adversary (believed to be Russia). This attack affected over 18,000 customers around the world and compromised multiple US and international government agencies. The full extent of the damage caused is still unknown, but it illustrates how devastating and wide-reaching nation-state cyberattacks can be, impacting businesses across various industries, including those in supply chains like defense or the military.[1]

Vaccine makers. During the COVID-19 pandemic, nation-state adversaries turned their attention to vaccine makers, conducting corporate sabotage and theft. This escalation shows that virtually no industry is immune to such attacks, including high-profile targets like financial institutions and critical national infrastructure providers.[2]

Intellectual property theft. China has been highlighted for making intellectual property theft a key part of its espionage efforts. This includes placing insiders in organizations to steal IP and targeting firms with malware and spear-phishing attacks.[3]

---

[1] Kate O'Flaherty, "The Nation State Threat to Business," ComputerWeekly, January 8, 2021. https://www.computer-weekly.com/feature/The-nation-state-threat-to-business.
[2] Ibid.
[3] Ibid.

Russian cyber operations. Russia's efforts are mainly focused on espionage and advancing Russian foreign policy, as opposed to commercial opportunities.[4]

Iranian cyberattacks. Iran has diversified its offensive cyber operations, including espionage, ransomware, and destructive cyberattacks. These have been some of the largest and most destructive, targeting nations like Saudi Arabia.[5]

North Korean financial attacks. North Korea's cyberattacks are largely financially motivated, targeting financial institutions and cryptocurrency platforms to compensate for economic sanctions against the country.[6]

These examples highlight the variety and severity of nation-state cyberattacks, underscoring the significant impact these attacks can have on businesses, sometimes leading to crippling fines, loss of investor confidence, and financial distress that can lead to a business's collapse.[7]

CYBERCRIMINALS
The group we all must worry most about is

---

[4] Ibid.
[5] Ibid.
[6] Ibid.
[7] Ibid.

cybercriminals. This is organized crime; it is big business. In fact, it is such big business that, as we mentioned earlier, cybercrime is now the "world's third-largest global economy" after the national economies of the United States and China.[8] That's incredible! Cybercriminals are making trillions of dollars every year.

Many cybercriminals operate as part of organized crime groups that are sophisticated and well-structured, resembling traditional organized crime syndicates in several ways:

Hierarchical structure. Cybercriminal groups often have a hierarchical structure with leaders, specialists, and lower-level operatives.

Specialization. Members often specialize in specific areas, such as hacking, phishing, malware distribution, or money laundering.

Global operations. Groups frequently operate internationally, exploiting the global nature of the internet to conduct crimes across borders.

---

[8] Justinas Vainilavičius, "Cybercrime Is World's Third-Largest Economy Thanks to Booming Black Market," Cybernews, November 15, 2023. https://cybernews.com/editorial/cybercrime-world-third-economy/.

Diverse criminal activities. Groups are involved in a variety of criminal activities, including identity theft, financial fraud, ransomware attacks, and the sale of illegal goods and services on the Dark Web.

Evasion techniques. Cybercriminals use advanced techniques to evade detection by law enforcement, including encrypted communication channels and laundering money through cryptocurrencies.

Recruitment and training. Groups often recruit skilled individuals and may provide training to develop specific cybercrime skills.

Financial motivation. The primary motivation for these groups is financial gain, though some may also be driven by political, ideological, or personal reasons.

Longevity and resilience. These groups can be persistent and adaptable, changing tactics as needed to avoid law enforcement and continue their activities.

However, not all cybercriminals are part of organized groups. There are also individual actors or small, less structured groups engaged in cybercrime. But the trend towards organization and sophistication is a significant concern for law enforcement and cybersecurity professionals.

Conclusion

Accurate, up-to-date statistics on the number of attacks specifically targeting individuals and families can be challenging to obtain, as many incidents go unreported. However, it's widely recognized that the number of attacks is significant and growing.

Be aware of the different types of cyberattacks—phishing, ransomware, identity theft, and others. I will discuss these in subsequent chapters. It is important to understand how these attacks are carried out, such as through email scams, unsecured internet connections, or malware.

When thinking about all these very skilled hackers at work 24 hours a day, what do you think is their primary method of attack? How are they getting into our systems and homes?

CHAPTER 2

The Fine Art of Phishing

A
ccording to a report by the respected SANS Institute of cybersecurity training and certification, 95 percent of all cyberattacks are a result of a successful phishing email.[9] This statistic highlights the significant risk from and prevalence of these types of cyberattacks involving the sending of deceptive emails that appear to come from a trusted source; they successfully trick individuals into revealing sensitive data or installing malware. The sophistication of these attacks is increasing, making it more challenging for individuals and businesses to protect themselves. Attacks are not limited to large, publicly traded companies. They have serious consequences for businesses of all sizes, as well as individuals and families.

---

[9] Neal Weinberg, "How to Blunt Spear Phishing Attacks," NetworkWorld, March 6, 2013. https://www.network-world.com/article/670302/how-to-blunt-spear-phishing-attacks.html.

Why Should I Care?

Phishing gets people to disclose sensitive information like usernames, passwords, and credit card details. Typically, phishing attacks are carried out via email, but they can also occur through other means, such as text messages, social media, phone calls, or fake websites.

The prevalence of phishing among cybercriminals is significant for several reasons:

Ease of deployment. Phishing attacks can be launched with relatively little technical skill compared to other types of cyberattacks. Thus, they appeal to a wide range of cybercriminals, from novices to more experienced hackers.

A very high success rate. Despite increased awareness, many people still fall for phishing scams. This is often due to sophisticated tactics, such as mimicking the look and feel of legitimate communications from well-known companies or organizations.

Versatility. Phishing can be used for a variety of malicious purposes, including stealing personal information, installing malware, or conducting corporate espionage. This makes it a favored tool in the arsenal of many cybercriminals.

Evolving techniques. Phishing continues to evolve, becoming more sophisticated and harder to detect, including targeted attacks known as spear-phishing (attackers customize their approach for specific individuals or organizations) and whaling (targeting high-profile individuals).

Economic advantage. For cybercriminals, the cost-benefit ratio is favorable. Phishing attacks are relatively inexpensive, especially compared to the potential profits from stolen data or compromised systems.

Quantifying exactly how much cybercriminals use phishing is challenging because many attacks go unreported, and methods constantly evolve. However, it's widely recognized in cybersecurity circles that phishing remains one of the most common and effective methods to compromise individuals and businesses alike.

Understanding the Issue

I will discuss businesses protecting themselves from phishing in Chapter 15. For now, I will cover guidelines for individuals and families.

Education and awareness are very important initial steps. Inform your entire family about what phishing is, what to look for, and why it is so vital to protect everyone from it.

In the past, it was easy to spot a phishing email

because of the poor grammar and spelling mistakes. While that can still be seen, the advent of artificial intelligence (AI) makes this less likely.

Using AI for creating phishing emails is a significant concern. Hackers can leverage it in several ways to target families:

Data collection. AI can analyze vast amounts of material about potential victims, like social media profiles, online activities, and public records. This allows for the creation of highly personalized and contextually relevant emails that appear more trustworthy.

Bespoke messaging. Using natural language processing (NLP), messages can be made more convincing. NLP can adapt language, tone, and style to match the communication patterns of the person or organization being impersonated.

Vulnerability detection. AI can help identify the most vulnerable targets in a household, such as children, older adults, or anyone with less cybersecurity training and awareness.

Just because an email contains specific facts about you or your family does not mean that it is a legitimate email. Hackers can gather a lot of data from the internet to trick people into thinking an email is legitimate and get them to open an attachment or click on a link.

Remember, it's important everyone takes the threat of phishing seriously. These attacks can lead to serious issues like identity theft or financial loss. Here are the top 10 warning signs:

1. **Suspicious source**. Check the email address carefully. It may be a slight variation on a legitimate one or completely unrelated to the supposed sender or organization.

2. **Urgent or threatening language**. Phishing emails often create a sense of urgency or fear, prompting quick action. They might threaten account closure, legal action, or other negative consequences.

3. **Unsolicited requests for personal information**. Legitimate organizations usually don't ask for sensitive data like passwords, social security numbers, or bank details via email.

4. **Generic greetings**. Phishing emails often use general greetings like "Dear Customer" instead of your actual name, indicating a mass email rather than a personal communication.

5. **Spelling and grammar errors**. As stated above, not all hackers are using AI. Spelling and grammar errors are still a red flag. Professional organizations typically send out well-written emails.

6. **Mismatched URLs**. Hover over links in the email (without clicking) to see the actual URL. If it doesn't match the context of the email or looks suspicious, it might be a phishing attempt.

7. **Unusual attachments**. Be very wary of unexpected email attachments, especially from unknown senders.

8. **Inconsistent design**. Look for inconsistencies in email formatting, logo quality, and overall design compared to previous communications from the same sender.

9. **Too-good-to-be-true offers**. Scams like the long-lost uncle who left you millions and the Nigerian prince who needs a wire transfer are still being used because, somehow, there are people who still fall to them.

10. **Request verification of account details**. Phishing emails may request clicking a link to verify your account details. Legitimate organizations don't ask for verification of sensitive data via email.

Practical Steps to Protect Against Phishing

Basically, always be cautious. Don't be too trusting and keep the following in mind:

Educate everyone about tactics used. It's essential that everyone understand what phishing is and how it works. Explain that it can occur through emails, text messages, social media messages, or phone calls, where scammers impersonate legitimate organizations to steal personal data.

Recognize suspicious emails and messages. Teach everyone to identify signs of phishing, such as misspellings, urgent or threatening language, and requests for personal information from the top 10 above.

Look closely at the <from> address. Hover the cursor over the <from> address or click on it to see who actually sent it.

Verify suspicious messages. If an email or message seems suspicious—even if it appears to come from a known contact or reputable organization—verify the identity of the requestor or sender through alternative means. Contact the organization or individual directly with a phone call, text message, or email known to be genuine. If you know the person, call or text them and ask if they sent the email. If it is from a business, do NOT click on any links and instead go to their website to seek information or call them at a number listed on the website—and not any number in the email.

Be cautious with links and attachments. Advise everyone not to click on links or download attachments from unknown or suspicious sources. This is a common phishing methodology for spreading malware or stealing data.

Enable two-factor authentication (2FA). Whenever possible, activate 2FA for all email accounts. This adds an additional layer of security, making it harder for attackers to gain access to accounts—even if they have the password. I will discuss 2FA in more detail in Chapter 5.

Use strong, unique email passwords. Encourage the use of complex, unique passwords for each account. Consider using a password manager to securely keep track of them. I will discuss this in more detail in Chapter 6.

Regularly monitor financial statements. Keep an eye on bank and credit card statements for any unauthorized transactions. This could be a sign of a successful phishing attack.

Report attempts. Educate everyone about how to report incidents. Most email services (Gmail, Outlook, etc.) have the option to report phishing directly within the email interface or application.

Remember, awareness and vigilance are key. Regular discussions and updates about cybersecurity can help keep every family member informed and prepared.

Additional Social Engineering Tactics

In addition to phishing, there are two other methods hackers like to use in their cyberattacks—smishing and vishing.

SMISHING

Ever received a text message from a number or someone you don't know? Sometimes it's innocuous like, "Hey, you are ten minutes late for the meeting. Are you coming?" Or maybe it's as simple as, "Hey is this Jane?" (and your name isn't Jane). This seems to happen to me multiple times a day. This is smishing.

"Smishing" is a form of cyberattack that involves sending fraudulent SMS (text) messages that are designed to trick people into revealing sensitive data or clicking on a link that downloads malicious software (malware) onto the phone being used. Smishing is a blend of "SMS" (short message service) and "phishing." Note that hackers will often use the names of legitimate, trusted businesses.

Here are five common types of smishing messages[10]:

---

[10] SecureWorld News Team, "5 Smishing Attack Examples Everyone Should See," SecureWorld, January 8, 2020. https://www.secureworld.io/industry-news/5-smishing-attack-examples-everyone-should-see.

Bank account lock alert. A message pretending to be from a bank alerting the recipient that their bank account is locked.

Credit card warning. This smishing attack claims to be from American Express, urgently notifying you about a credit card issue.

Prize-winning notification. A smishing message from a source claiming to be Walmart, indicating that the recipient has won a prize and needs to click a link to claim it.

Fake survey lure. Posing as Amazon, recipients are enticed with the promise of a prize for taking a survey.

Unusual account activity alert. Masquerading as Apple Support, a message warns of unusual account activity and prompts the user to click a link to secure their information.

Order issue. A message purporting to be from FedEx, UPS, DHL, etc., stating that there is a problem with your shipment and to click on the link for more information.

These attacks often rely on creating a sense of urgency or offering enticing rewards that can lead to infected devices and compromised data.

Key points about dealing with smishing:

Legitimate source. Smishing messages often appear to be from legitimate sources, such as banks, government agencies, or familiar service providers.

Urgency. These messages typically create a sense of urgency, prompting quick action like clicking on a link or providing data or documents immediately.

An offer. Offers that seem too good to be true.

Be skeptical. Always be cautious of unsolicited messages, especially those requesting personal information.

Verify the source. If a message claims to be from a known organization, independently verify it through official channels.

Never click links. Avoid clicking on links in text messages, especially if they're from unknown or suspicious sources.

Report suspicious smishing. Androids and iPhones have a feature to Report and Delete a message. If the number is not in your contacts, there will be a Report and Delete link at the very bottom when the message is opened.

Blocking. The number used in the smishing can be blocked, though usually using the Report and Delete feature will be sufficient.

Staying vigilant, regularly updating your knowledge of cybersecurity issues, and following these best practices can significantly reduce the risk of falling victim to smishing scams.

VISHING

Ever received a phone call purporting to be from some organization asking a lot of questions?

In one of my previous organizations, a fraudster called two separate offices asking to speak with Mary. The interesting thing is they had Mary's actual company ID number. We didn't know how they got it, but they had it and were trying to get her full name, email, phone, and other data. But our employees were well-trained, hung up, and reported the number to security.

This is vishing.

A combination of "voice" and "phishing," this is a type of scam where fraudsters use phone calls to trick individuals into divulging sensitive information. The scammers often pose as representatives from legitimate organizations—banks, government agencies, or tech support companies—to gain the victim's trust.

Defenses against vishing:

Be skeptical of unsolicited calls. If contacted by someone claiming to be from a company or government agency, be cautious. It's wise to assume that any unsolicited call is a scam.

Verify caller's identity. If a caller requests personal information, verify their identity. Hang up and call the organization they claim to represent. Use a phone number from their official website or account statements, not the number the caller provides.

Do not share personal data. Never share personal, financial, or sensitive information over the phone unless you initiated the call and are certain of the recipient's identity.

Use call-blocking tools. Phone service providers or third-party apps can block and reduce the number of unwanted calls.

Stay informed. Be aware of common vishing tactics and stay updated on new scamming techniques. Scammers are constantly evolving.

Report suspicious calls. If receiving a suspicious call, report it to the relevant authorities, such as your phone company, the Federal Trade Commission (FTC), or other consumer protection agencies.

Educate others. Share knowledge about vishing scams with friends and family, especially those who may be more vulnerable, like the elderly.

Vishing has been used in various sophisticated attacks to gain unauthorized access to systems and sensitive information.

X (FORMERLY TWITTER) VISHING ATTACK

One notable example is the attack on Twitter in July 2020. Posing as Twitter IT staff, employees were contacted in order to gain access to Twitter's internal systems. The attackers specifically targeted certain employees who had access to account support tools, then convinced them that they were from the IT department and needed credentials for a system check or update. Through these conversations, the attackers gained credentials or persuaded employees to enter their credentials into a webpage controlled by the attackers.

The attackers took control of several high-profile Twitter accounts, including those of Elon Musk, Barack Obama, and Bill Gates. They then posted messages promoting a scam, which tricked users into sending money to the attacker's bitcoin wallet.

This was a significant attack because of the high profile of the targeted accounts and the direct financial implications. It prompted a reevaluation of security protocols at Twitter and highlighted the vulnerabilities that even tech-savvy organizations face against social engineering attacks. This incident underscored the need for comprehensive training for employees on recognizing and responding to such attacks. It also emphasized the importance of robust security measures like multifactor authentication to prevent unauthorized access.

This example demonstrates how vishing—by combining elements of social engineering and traditional hacking—can lead to significant breaches in security that can affect even major tech companies.

THE IT COMPANY SCAM

Another example has happened to many individuals, families, and small businesses. The fraudster calls, claiming to be from a reputable IT company's tech support team. They mention a fictitious but convincing cybersecurity threat that is affecting businesses (or families) in the area. The caller uses technical jargon and references recent real-world cybersecurity incidents to sound knowledgeable and urgent.

They convince the person that immediate action is needed to secure their systems. The person is guided to downloading a remote desktop tool under the guise of allowing "tech support" to assist them. Once the tool is installed, the cybercriminal gains remote access to the system. Moving quickly, they bypass security protocols under the pretense of conducting security checks and instead access confidential information, including customer data, financial records, and login credentials for various services.

Before ending the call, the fraudster installs additional malware to ensure continued access to the system, resulting in significant financial losses.

These examples illustrate the sophistication of vishing attacks and their potential to cause substantial harm to families and small businesses. Regular training and awareness are crucial.

Conclusion

Remember, legitimate organizations will never demand immediate action, use scare tactics, demand sensitive information over the phone, or ask for passwords or PINs (personal identification numbers). Always take your time to verify the legitimacy of the call. Protecting against phishing, smishing, and vishing is critical due to their potential to cause significant harm, both personally and professionally.

Phishing, which often involves deceptive emails to steal sensitive data, can lead to identity theft, financial loss, and unauthorized access to personal or corporate networks. Smishing, or SMS phishing, uses text messages to trick recipients into revealing personal data or downloading malware, posing risks similar to email phishing. Vishing, or voice phishing, employs phone calls to deceitfully obtain confidential information, often targeting the elderly or less tech-savvy individuals.

These tactics not only compromise individual security but can also have broader impacts, such as damaging an organization's reputation or leading to extensive financial and data breaches. Therefore, awareness and preventive measures against these social engineering attacks are essential to safeguard personal and organizational assets and maintain trust and security in digital communications.

CHAPTER 3

Email Is the Best Way In

How do hackers get our information with these phishing attacks? It typically starts with an easily available email address. And why is that? Because many people use their full name in their email addresses. So, once they have your full name, hackers only have to do a little additional research to find out more.

If like most people, there's a good chance you have two or more email addresses with your first and last name in it. Many of us have a work email that has either <firstnamelastname@ourbusiness.com> or maybe <firstinitiallastname@ourbusiness.com>. Then a personal email <firstnamelastname@Gmail/Hotmail/Yahoo>. Maybe you still use that alma mater email <firsnamelastname@yourschool.edu>.

Make Email Best Practices Routine

One thing I suggest is only using your work email only for business communications. Do not use it for things like hotels, airlines, ridesharing apps, etc. So many of these businesses have been hacked and will be again. A really good example is the large international hotel chain JW Marriott, which had a major cyber breach in 2018,[11] another in 2020,[12] and yet another in 2022.[13] Three times in five years.

The reason this happens is because these businesses provide a wealth of data. When hackers get in, they start googling the names attached to all the stolen accounts. When they find one who appears to be a successful individual, that person goes high up on their target list. Or maybe they find a business that appears to have a lot of revenue; now, they have the name of someone inside that business and that individual goes on the target list.

---

[11] Associated Press, "Marriott Says 5.2 Million Guests Affected in 2nd Data Breach in Just Over a Year," CBC, March 31, 2020. https://www.cbc.ca/news/business/marriott-data-breach-worldwide-1.5516652.

[12] Catalin Cimpanu, "Marriott Discloses New Data Breach Impacting 5.2 Million Hotel Guests," ZDNET, March 31, 2020. https://www.zdnet.com/article/marriott-discloses-new-data-breach-impacting-5-2-million-hotel-guests/.

[13] Carly Page, "Hotel Giant Marriott Confirms Yet Another Data Breach," TechCrunch, July 6, 2022.
https://techcrunch.com/2022/07/06/marriott-breach-again/.

So only use a business email for communications that are strictly business-related.

Similarly, wean yourself off <firstnamelastname> at Gmail or Hotmail or Yahoo. Don't use that address for everything. Keep it for just the people you know and trust.

What next? Create and use anonymous email addresses for many activities, which I'll get to below. But first, let me cover some additional methods hackers use:

Data breaches. Unfortunately, most of us have had personal information involved in a big-company incident. One common method of hackers is to breach a company, steal as much personal material as possible (names, addresses, email addresses, phone numbers), and then use it in subsequent attacks or sell it on the criminal marketplace. If that info were to be part of a cyber breach, would it include your email address?

On the Dark Web, hackers can purchase thousands upon thousands of records that were part of a data breach.

Publicly available information. Email addresses can be scraped from public websites or social media platforms where individuals might have shared contact info. When setting up an account on an online platform or a social media site, make sure the email address is hidden from public access. If you have a personal website, it's best practice to use a generic email address rather than having the primary one exposed in public.

Phishing scams. Ironically, phishing emails themselves can be a source of data for hackers. If someone responds to one, their email address is confirmed as active and they may be targeted even more. The same thing occurs when someone responds to a smishing text. Now the hackers know the number goes to a person who might fall for their attack.

Purchased lists. Hackers can buy lists of email addresses from other cybercriminals or illegitimate marketing firms. There are over 4,000 data broker companies on the internet to be scoured looking for information. I will discuss identity theft further in Chapter 12.

Guessing and generation. Hackers sometimes use common naming conventions (like <john.doe@example.com>) to generate potential email addresses, then send phishing emails to them. For example, if social media profiles announce your first and last name, then hackers will send an email to <firstname.lastname> at Gmail or Hotmail. Social media privacy and security protections are covered later in the book, but other than LinkedIn there's no reason to use a real name on social media.

Spyware or malware. One other way hackers get email addresses and other data is through malicious software, known as malware. When installed on a computer it can capture email addresses and other personal info. Chapter 10 will cover protection using antivirus and anti-malware software.

To reduce the risk of an email address being targeted, consider the following steps:

STAY ANONYMOUS ONLINE

Keep that <firstname.lastname@gmail.com> only for people you know and trust. For all others, create anonymous email addresses.

For example, <iloverunning@gmail>. What can be gleaned from that? Not the name, gender, age, race, or anything else about the person using it (the person may not even love running). It is an email address that hackers would throw away because it's of no use to them.

And if it gets exposed in a cyber breach, then just stop using it and create a new one like <ihatewalking@gmail>. If you are not a creative person, many major email providers offer anonymous email addresses for free. Sometimes it takes some searching to find this feature but it's usually available.

VARIETY IS THE SPICE OF LIFE...AND SAFER

I've worked with many people who only have one

email address. They use it for everything. If you are one of those people, please make at least one anonymous email. Get away from using an email that includes your name. This might sound like a daunting task—changing contact info on every online account—but get into the habit of logging in and changing the email address for that account when visiting a website. Gradually this will increase cyber hygiene.

And I suggest having separate ones for different purposes—maybe one for online shopping, another for social media, another for travel sites (airlines, hotels, ridesharing apps, etc.).

Be Cautious About Sharing

Always be mindful of where and how you share an email address, especially on public platforms.

Conclusion

Defending email addresses is crucial because they often serve as a gateway to our digital identity. Email accounts are frequently linked to various other online accounts, including social media, banking, and shopping sites. This makes them a prime target for hackers.

A compromised email can lead to identity theft, financial loss, and unauthorized access to sensitive personal data. Using anonymous email addresses, especially for online activities that don't require personal information, helps maintain privacy and security. This will reduce the risk of spam, phishing attacks, and potential breaches. By keeping a primary email address more secure and less exposed to public domains, your overall online security posture is enhanced and there is better protection from cyber threats.

CHAPTER 4

Ransomware

Ransomware attacks can target families, although they are more commonly aimed at businesses and organizations due to their ability to pay larger ransoms (ransomware issues for businesses will be discussed in Chapter 16). But I want to emphasize that individual users, including families, are not immune to these attacks. Ransomware can infect a personal computer or a home network, leading to the encryption of personal files, photos, and important documents. In such cases, the attackers demand a ransom, usually in cryptocurrency, to unlock the files.

Such attacks can happen in several different ways, but the primary infection method is usually through a successful phishing attack.

Do I Really Need to Worry About This?

Let's take one example. A married couple in Pennsylvania fell victim to a ransomware attack that encrypted the systems on their home network. They felt violated. And if they didn't pay the ransom, they would lose all the pictures and videos of their three young children, not to mention tax files, bank statements, and other data. The financial records could probably be recovered from the businesses involved, but the joyous memories of their children weren't stored anywhere else. They paid an $8,000 ransom in cryptocurrency.

Families can protect themselves from ransomware in several ways:

Regular backups. Keep regular backups of important files so that, even if your files are externally encrypted, there are copies stored elsewhere. It's crucial these backups are not connected to the network or main device. Use a removable hard drive or online systems like Google Drive or Microsoft's OneDrive, which are cloud-based systems that back up data in near real time. Both have security features to help prevent ransomware attacks.

Software updates. Regularly update all software, including operating systems and antivirus programs, to defend against known vulnerabilities that hackers have learned to exploit.

Caution with emails and links. Be cautious about clicking on links or opening email attachments from unknown or suspicious sources. Many ransomware attacks start with a phishing email.

Use antivirus and anti-malware software. Install and maintain reliable security software to detect and prevent ransomware attacks.

Education. Ensure that all family members are aware of the risks of ransomware and know how to recognize suspicious emails and links.

Conclusion

There have been numerous instances where individuals have shared their experiences of falling victim to such attacks, often including the loss of personal photos and documents. There is an emotional toll from such attacks. These experiences serve as reminders that everyone is potentially at risk and should take proactive measures to defend their digital lives.

Ransomware is a type of malicious software that encrypts a victim's files, making them inaccessible, and then demands a ransom payment to restore access. Protecting against it is crucial. The impacts of ransomware attacks are far-reaching: loss of critical personal, financial, or business information; disruption of business operations; financial losses; and comprised sensitive data. For businesses, this can mean a loss of reputation and customer trust. Furthermore, paying the ransom does not always guarantee that access will be restored.

Effective measures to prevent ransomware attacks, such as regular backups, updates, system patches, and employee education, are essential to safeguarding digital assets and maintaining the integrity and continuity of operations.

CHAPTER 5

The Single Best Way to Protect Everything: 2FA

One of the most effective things to do to protect accounts, both personal and business, is to use two-factor authentication (2FA). It's also called multifactor authentication (MFA), while some sites call it two-step verification. As described earlier, use two-factor authentication for email. But banking sites and banking apps? Absolutely! I also suggest turning it on anywhere and everywhere it is offered.

Two-factor authentication is a security process in which users must provide two different authentication factors to be verified. This better defends both the user's credentials and the resources a user can access. 2FA adds an additional layer of security to the authentication process. This makes it harder for attackers to gain access to devices or online accounts because just knowing the victim's password is not enough to get past the authentication check.

The two factors involved typically include something you know (like a password or PIN), something you have (like a smartphone or a security token), and/or something you are that is part of you (like a fingerprint or other biometric data).

Two-factor authentication is very common already, like logging onto a website and getting a multi-digit code via text that must then be entered. But websites are getting away from this method because hackers are developing the capability to exploit vulnerabilities in SMS (text messages) and intercepting this code (I'll describe this in more detail later when I discuss mobile device takeover schemes).

Don't Let SMS Codes Get Intercepted

Hacking into accounts via intercepted SMS codes is a real and growing concern in the cybersecurity world. What happens is that a hacker identifies a target, usually someone with valuable data or access, like a high-profile individual or someone with administrative access to sensitive systems. Then they gather information about the target (phone numbers, email addresses, and other personal details), often obtained through social engineering, phishing, or previous breaches. The hacker then employs various methods to intercept SMS codes. The two most common are:

SIM swapping. The hacker convinces an employee of a mobile phone provider to transfer the victim's phone number to a SIM card (cell phone) in their possession. Once the number is transferred, all SMS messages, including 2FA codes, are sent to the hacker's phone.

Phishing attacks. The hacker tricks the user into revealing their 2FA codes directly. Once the hacker has the SMS code, they can quickly use it to complete the 2FA process and gain access to the user's account. This could be a bank account, email, social media, or any other service that uses SMS-based 2FA.

After gaining access, the hacker can steal sensitive data, transfer funds, send out phishing messages from the compromised account, or even lock the legitimate user out of their own account.

Skilled hackers will attempt to cover their tracks by deleting logs, using a virtual private network (VPN), and employing other methods to avoid detection.

These scenarios underscore the importance of using more secure methods of 2FA that are less susceptible to interception compared to SMS-based 2FA, like biometrics, authenticator apps, or hardware tokens. Additionally, it highlights the need for continuous vigilance and continuing education about cybersecurity threats and best practices.

If a hacker can guess or crack your password, then having two-factor authentication turned on will prevent the hacker from being able to log into your account. By requiring a second form of identification, 2FA makes it significantly more difficult to impersonate a user and gain access to computers, accounts, or other sensitive resources.

The Best 2FA Methods

BIOMETRICS

Biometric authentication uses unique physical characteristics of an individual to verify their identity. Common methods include fingerprint scanning, facial recognition, iris or retina scanning, and voice recognition. However, biometrics aren't foolproof. They can be tricked (though it's very difficult) and, unlike a password, if compromised you can't change them.

The advantages of biometrics are: 1) high security (they are unique to each individual and difficult to replicate or steal) and 2) convenience (users don't have to remember passwords or carry additional devices).

The disadvantages are: potential privacy concerns. Biometric data is sensitive, and some people do not want it stored by third parties. Also, some systems might struggle with accuracy in different conditions (e.g., poor lighting for facial recognition).

AUTHENTICATOR APPS

These apps generate a time-sensitive code on a user's mobile device. Popular examples include

Google Authenticator, Microsoft Authenticator, and Authy.

The advantages are these are more secure than SMS-based 2FA since they are less susceptible to interception or SIM-swapping attacks. They are convenient for users who have a smartphone. The disadvantage is dependence on a device. If a phone is lost, stolen, out of power, or used internationally, access can be problematic. Also, not everyone has a smartphone.

HARDWARE TOKENS

These are physical devices (like a USB key or a small fob) that generate a passcode or use a push button to authenticate a login. YubiKey is a well-known example.

The advantages are they are not connected to the internet and are thus less vulnerable to remote attacks. They are easy to use, often requiring just a button to press or a USB slot. The disadvantages are they can be lost or damaged and replacing them can be costly. They also add the inconvenience of carrying an extra device.

Conclusion

Each authentication method has its strengths and weaknesses, so each is suitable for different scenarios and user preferences. The choice often depends on the balance between the desired level of security and convenience for the user.

While 2FA significantly enhances security, its strength depends on the methods used. SMS-based 2FA, though common, has vulnerabilities that can be exploited, whereas biometrics, authenticator apps, or hardware tokens offer a more secure, albeit not infallible, convenient alternative. The 2FA method should balance security needs, convenience, and potential risks.

Two-factor authentication is critically important to enhance online security and protecting personal and sensitive information. It operates by requiring two different forms of identification before granting access to an account or system. This approach significantly reduces the risk of unauthorized access. By adding this extra layer of security, 2FA helps safeguard against various cyber threats like phishing, identity theft, and breaches. In a digital age where personal data can be highly valuable and vulnerable, its importance is hard to exaggerate. Thus, 2FA is a vital tool for maintaining the integrity and confidentiality of digital accounts.

CHAPTER 6

That Was the Password You Just Used!

The next biggest issue regarding the safety of accounts is very weak passwords, whether we're talking about online accounts, home systems and networks, or even mobile devices. Look at this list of the top 10 most hacked passwords in the United States in 2024. Hope yours is not on the list. But if these are the ten most hacked passwords, then that means many, many people are still using these weak, easily hackable obstacles:

123456. Cited as the most commonly used password, reflecting its simplicity and lack of security.

password. Also shows the tendency of users to opt for extremely basic passwords.

123456789. It's not that hard for hackers to add the next three numbers onto the list's number one.

qwerty123. This password is based on the first six letters found in the top row of a standard keyboard.

secret. Dictionary words are very easy to crack.

iloveyou. This will make hackers love you too.

letmein. That's what they want, now isn't it?

football. Sports tend to be common passwords and very easily cracked.

princess. This has been among the top 10 for many years.

monkey. Animals and pet names are also commonly used as passwords.

These passwords highlight the ongoing issue of users choosing convenience over security—and making their accounts vulnerable to hacking. More complex and unique passwords will enhance security.

Cracking the Code Isn't That Hard

The speed at which a hacker can crack the code using a password-hacking tool depends on various factors, including the complexity of the password, the strength of the hashing algorithm used (if any), and the computing power of the hacker's system. Here are a few key points to consider:

SIMPLE DICTIONARY ATTACKS

If the password is a common dictionary word, it can be cracked **almost instantly** using a simple dictionary attack, which uses a pre-compiled list of common words and tries them one by one until getting a hit.

COMPUTING POWER

The more computing power the attacker has, the faster they can attempt different passwords. With powerful hardware or a botnet,[14] an attacker can try millions of passwords per second.

PASSWORD HASHING

If the password is stored in a hashed (encrypted) form, the time to crack it depends on the hashing algorithm. Stronger algorithms like bcrypt, scrypt, or

---

[14] A botnet is a network of computers that have been infected by malware, which allows them to be controlled remotely by an attacker, often without the knowledge of the computer owners.

Argon2 are designed to be computationally intensive and, thus, slow down brute-force attacks.

PASSWORD LENGTH AND COMPLEXITY

Longer passwords and those with a mix of characters (uppercase, lowercase, numbers, and symbols) take longer to crack. However, a single dictionary word, even with mixed cases, is generally weak.

So, a simple password can be cracked in a matter of seconds or minutes, especially if no strong hashing algorithm or additional security measures (like salting, which is a way to randomize a password) are in use. To enhance security, do what's recommended: Use longer, more complex passwords and multifactor authentication where possible.

How Long Does a Password Really Need to Be?

Are you ready? **A password should be a minimum of 16 characters!**

I can hear the groaning. But this is the reality, plus there are ways to create a 16-character password that actually is easy to remember.

Hackers, using today's technologies, cannot crack passwords that are 16 sixteen or more characters. To crack one composed of only lowercase letters using a brute-force attack with a system capable of making 1 billion guesses per second, it would theoretically take:

- 43.61×102143.61×1021 total combinations, taking
- 43.61×101243.61×1012 seconds, or
- 504.73504.73 million days, or
- about 1.38 million years!

These calculations show that even a relatively simple 16-character password (lowercase letters only) would require an impractically long time to crack with brute-force methods. The time required is exponentially increased if the password includes uppercase letters, numbers, and symbols. This demonstrates the effectiveness of longer passwords.

There are very large organizations, including many in the financial services industry, that have switched to 16-character passwords for their employees—who were not, at first, happy about it. But then they realized the advantage: 16-character passwords cannot be cracked, so there are no complexity requirements. The password can be all lowercase and an easy phrase, like <ilovetogorunning>.

Another thing big companies did was require employees to change passwords every 90 days. We should all have been doing this, too, though obviously most people don't. But since 16-character passwords cannot be cracked, changing passwords periodically doesn't need to happen.

One by one, start changing your accounts to 16-character passphrases. On personal systems and networks, it's alright to use an all-lowercase one.

However, many websites mandate the use of upper and lowercase letters, numbers, and special characters. For those sites, add a little complexity. For example, <Iloverunning4fun>.

Here's a technique I hinted at earlier. Have an eight-character complex password that you've used for years and now remember very well? Then, just type it twice and there's your 16-character, easy-to-remember password. Instead of <Hot2023!>, start using <Hot2023!Hot2023!>. Voilà, an uncrackable password.

The Easy Way to Manage Passwords

One of the best ways to manage all very long and very complex passwords is by using a password manager application. This is a software tool designed to securely store, manage, and organize passwords and other sensitive information. Here are some key features and benefits of them:

SECURE STORAGE

Password managers encrypt passwords and sensitive data, providing a secure vault that can only be accessed with a master password. This is much safer than using a notebook or unsecured digital document. As discussed previously, a master password should be at least 16 or more characters and contain all four complexity requirements.

Also save things like a friend's name, phone

number, email address, or other personal information in these secure vaults so they are fully encrypted and safe.

PASSWORD GENERATION

Password manager applications can generate strong, unique passwords for multiple accounts. These passwords are usually 20, 22, or 24 characters in length and very complex. But you never have to remember any of them. The password manager does that. This helps to maintain high-security standards without needing to remember complex passwords.

AUTOFILL FEATURE

Most password managers integrate with the latest internet browsers and offer an autofill feature for online forms. This not only speeds up logging onto websites but also reduces the risk of typing errors. This autofill feature also works when changing passwords on a website. To the right of the box where the password is entered, just click on the password manager button. It fills in a long complex password and then saves it in the password manager application.

CROSS-PLATFORM COMPATABILITY

Password manager applications often work across different devices and platforms, ensuring access to passwords whether using a PC, smartphone, or tablet.

SINGLE MASTER PASSWORD

You only need to remember one master password to access all stored credentials. This master password should be 16 or more characters and use all four complexity requirements—upper and lowercase letters, numbers, and special characters.

SECURE SHARING

Some password managers allow the secure sharing of passwords with others, which is useful for families or work teams.

TWO-FACTOR AUTHENTICATION

Make sure that a password manager that provides 2FA is selected because this will add that extra layer of security.

AUDIT FEATURES

Password manager applications often include features to audit passwords, notifying you of weak, reused, or old passwords that need updating.

Research the top password manager applications. Some offer trial periods that will allow you to get used to them. Once an application is chosen, get an annual plan (some include family plans). Then just download the application to each device; you only need one account but install the app on all of them. The application syncs everything in the cloud.

Using a password manager application reduces the risk of password theft and improves overall online security. It's a valuable tool in a world where the number and complexity of passwords are constantly increasing.

Conclusion

Using complex passwords or a password manager is crucial for digital security. Complex passwords, which combine upper and lowercase letters, numbers, and special characters in an unpredictable sequence, are significantly harder for cyberattackers to guess or crack through brute-force methods and nearly impossible if 16 or more characters are used. Simple or commonly used passwords can be easily compromised, leading to unauthorized access to personal and sensitive information.

Password managers further enhance security by securely storing a variety of complex passwords, which eliminates the need to remember each one. They also often generate strong, unique passwords for each account, reducing the risk of multiple accounts being compromised if one password is breached. Additionally, password managers can help in detecting and preventing phishing attempts by autofilling credentials only on recognized sites.

Overall, the use of complex passwords and password managers plays a vital role in safeguarding online identities and sensitive data against growing cyber threats.

CHAPTER 7

Can They Hack My Home Wi-Fi?

Many of my clients believed their Wi-Fi routers were plug-and-play and automatically secure. Some believed that their internet service provider (ISP) was protecting them against hacking. Both theories are incorrect.

Home Wi-Fi networks, like any other network, are vulnerable if not properly secured. Hackers can exploit weaknesses for various malicious activities, such as stealing personal information, conducting surveillance, or using the network for illegal activities (becoming part of their botnet or even for crypto mining).

Why Wouldn't They Hack Your Home Wi-Fi Network?

Hackers are constantly scanning the internet looking for vulnerabilities. And they do not have to be halfway around the world. They can be right there in your hometown, using a technique called "war driving." Yes, this is a practice that some hackers still engage in.

The term originates from "war dialing," a method popularized in the 1980s when hackers would dial sequential phone numbers to find modems. War driving is the same concept applied to wireless networks. Here's why hackers do it:

Discovery of open networks. Hackers use war driving to identify open or poorly secured Wi-Fi networks. They often drive around neighborhoods or commercial areas with a laptop or other mobile device equipped with Wi-Fi scanning tools.

Exploiting security vulnerabilities. Once a vulnerable network is found, hackers exploit its weaknesses. This could be for unauthorized internet access, launching attacks on other networks, or conducting illegal activities anonymously.

Data theft. Unsecured or poorly secured networks can be a goldmine for hackers. Their targets can include passwords, financial information, or sensitive corporate intelligence. Since COVID-19, many people are still working from home remotely. This can provide hackers access to that business.

Counter Defenses

Here are some common vulnerabilities and the best ways to properly protect them. These might seem a little bit technical, but they are easy to configure. Most modern home Wi-Fi routers have an easy browser-based configuration page with instructions.

DEFAULT OR WEAK PASSWORDS

People often don't realize how important it is to change the default passwords on their Wi-Fi router. Hackers can query a Wi-Fi router and discover the make and model, then go on the internet and find the default password for that router. Change the default password.

Another related issue is changing the password but choosing one for its convenience that is, however, too weak. As previously discussed, easily guessable passwords can be quickly cracked by hackers. Create strong passwords for a home network.

SECURITY PROTOCOLS

The strongest encryption protocol currently available for home Wi-Fi routers is WPA3 (Wi-Fi Protected Access 3). It is the most secure protocol for home wireless networks. Also consider disabling the earlier WPS (Wi-Fi Protected Setup) that has weaker security.

USE A SECOND OR "GUEST" NETWORK

It is important to set up two networks for home Wi-Fi. The first is the main network where personal, sensitive, financial, and other information is located. The devices of trusted family members, as well as devices like printers, go on this main network.

The guest network is for everything else. Whether friends or other visitors who want to connect to Wi-Fi, they go on the guest network.

I suggest putting school-age children on the guest network as well. The reason is that children love to engage in online gaming activities or browse questionable websites that their parents might not know about. Online gaming sites are well-known to have hackers trying to either hack the game or hack other players.

I had a client a few years ago. I had gone through all the things in this book to help defend their household. About two months after reviewing everything with them, they called in a panic. They had a 14-year-old daughter who was a big-time online gamer. The parents told me they did everything else except the second Wi-Fi network because it was a little more technical and they weren't sure how to do it. The daughter was playing one of her online games on the main network. Her gaming account was hacked, and the parents were in a panic that the hackers would get to their financials. This happens often.

INTERNET OF THINGS (IOT)

Additionally—and this is quite important—there may be dozens of internet-connected devices in a modern home. These are things like a smart TV that connects to streaming movie services or a smart refrigerator that tells you the milk and eggs are getting low. It might be convenience devices like Alexa, Ring, Google Nest, and similar gadgets or home automation devices that are controlled via an app. Even exercise equipment is often connected to the outside world now. Many of these devices have been hacked in the past and will probably be hacked again. This is why all those devices should be on the guest network so hackers can't get on the main network and eventually find profitable intelligence to steal.

WI-FI NETWORK NAMES

Give the main and guest networks nondescript names. Do not use your address, family name, or anything that hackers could use. On the guest network, do not use the word guest. If a hacker sees that, they will look harder to find the main network because they know that's where the information is that they want.

TURN OFF NETWORK NAME BROADCASTING

Some security professionals believe that Wi-Fi network names should be hidden. But the reality is that hackers have scanning tools that let them see hidden networks. The list of networks shown by their scanning tool will include those that do not have a name, which might make them quite curious as to why this network is being hidden. You are better off just giving the networks nondescript names.

OUTDATED FIRMWARE

Older firmware may have unpatched security flaws that hackers can exploit. Most modern Wi-Fi routers have an auto-update feature. Make sure that is turned on.

FIREWALL AND NETWORK MONITORING

Most modern home Wi-Fi routers have a built-in firewall for network monitoring. Just make sure it is turned on and use the default configurations to monitor network activity for unusual behavior.

Conclusion

Securing a Wi-Fi network is a continuous process. New vulnerabilities can and do emerge. Regularly reviewing and updating security practices is essential for maintaining a safe network environment. Also, because technologies change so frequently, it's good practice to change a home Wi-Fi router every three years. Not only will they have the latest security protocols, but they are also much faster than the older ones.

Securing a home Wi-Fi network is crucial for

several reasons: 1) it protects personal and sensitive information from unauthorized access because unsecured networks are vulnerable to cyberattacks; 2) securing a network prevents unauthorized usage that can slow down internet access speeds and, if there are data limits, lead to usage charges; and 3) it helps safeguard devices connected to the network from malware and other cyber threats.

All of this contributes to the overall cybersecurity environment. Compromised home networks can be used as launch points for large-scale attacks on other networks. In summary, proper Wi-Fi security is vital for defending personal information, ensuring optimal network performance, and contributing to broader cybersecurity efforts.

CHAPTER 8

The Dangers of Public Wi-Fi

Public Wi-Fi networks are, broadly, any Wi-Fi networks outside of your protected home or office network. Some common places you might find a public network are libraries; cybercafes; coffee and other shops with free Wi-Fi; restaurants; hotels; and public transportation.

Due to their open nature, public networks are often targets for hackers. Be very cautious using public Wi-Fi. While convenient, it is inherently dangerous and it's crucial to take steps to protect data and privacy. Using a virtual private network, avoiding sensitive transactions, and adhering to good security practices can significantly reduce the risks associated with using public Wi-Fi.

A notable real-world example occurred in 2018

when a technique known as Evil Twin was used to attack a popular coffee chain. The hackers set up a fake Wi-Fi network that mimicked the legitimate one. Unsuspecting customers connected to the fake Wi-Fi. Once connected, the hackers intercepted what was being transmitted, including personal information, login credentials, credit card records, and other sensitive data.

This attack was sophisticated and well-coordinated. It highlights the risks associated with public Wi-Fi networks. The rogue network operated seamlessly, and users were unaware that something was amiss. The incident served as a wake-up call for both users and businesses, emphasizing the need for better security measures for public Wi-Fi networks.

What Can Go Wrong

There are several ways that logging on in public can go sideways:

UNENCRYPTED CONNECTIONS

Public Wi-Fi networks often lack robust security protocols. This means that even basic defenses are not in place, making them hotspots for malicious activities. Many do not encrypt data—meaning no hypertext transfer protocol secure (HTTPS) protection—so what is being sent and received is out in the open. Hackers can capture and analyze network traffic, then intercept unencrypted data.

Since nothing is encrypted, it's relatively easy for someone to intercept it, including personal information, emails, login credentials, website visits, financial details, etc. This can lead to identity theft and compromised business communications.

FAKE WI-FI NETWORKS

As mentioned earlier, cybercriminals often set up rogue Wi-Fi networks with legitimate-sounding names that trick users into connecting to them, enabling the theft of data.

For example, one letter in the legitimate network's name is changed, or "free" is added to the end of it. Connecting to the fake Wi-Fi network still gets you on the internet, where hackers want you. They can now use keystroke monitoring to capture when you're logging onto a website with a specific username and password.

MAN-IN-THE-MIDDLE ATTACKS

A similar type of attack intercepts data transmitted over unencrypted or poorly secured networks. A man-in-the-middle attack on public Wi-Fi typically involves a hacker secretly intercepting—and possibly altering—communication between two parties who believe they are only communicating with each other.

First, the attacker positions themselves between the victim's device and the Wi-Fi network. Public networks are particularly vulnerable because they often lack strong security measures. Using a rogue Wi-Fi access point that looks legitimate, the attacker then intercepts whatever is being transmitted between the user's device and the network.

The attacker can intercept, read, and modify any data passing through and extract valuable information. They can also alter it before it reaches its intended destination, potentially sending malicious links or disinformation. In some cases, the attacker might hijack an active session, like a logged-in email or social media session, to gain unauthorized access to the user's accounts.

MALWARE DISTRIBUTION

Hackers can use unsecured Wi-Fi to distribute malware to any device connected to the network, typically in conjunction with one of the above types of attacks.

Public Wi-Fi Best Practices

When out and about and needing to connect to the internet, the best thing to do is to use a cell phone hotspot. Go into your settings, find the personal hotspot, and turn it on, making sure it is password-protected. Next, connect the laptop or tablet to this personal hotspot; the resulting connection is with your cell phone provider and is completely encrypted. Another advantage is that, with a 5G cell phone and a strong connection, the connection is much faster than with standard Wi-Fi.

But in reality, cellular signals being what they are, there might be times when there's no choice but to use public Wi-Fi. In such circumstances, go ahead and connect to public Wi-Fi. But the first thing to do is set up a personal virtual private network (VPN). There are many very reputable VPN applications available. Go online, find one, purchase an annual subscription, and then download the VPN app to all devices.

VPNs ensure that the connection from a device to a website is completely encrypted and defended. It is good practice to have the VPN running on devices at all times. Even at home, it is good to have a VPN on to protect the connection to the internet.

Here are a few other best practices when connecting to public Wi-Fi:

Ensure websites are HTTPS. Before entering any sensitive information onto a website, ensure that it is using HTTPS, which signifies a secure, encrypted connection. To check HTTPS status, look for the lock symbol at the beginning of the URL (website address) at the top of the browser.

Avoid sensitive transactions. Avoid online banking, shopping, or any other similar transaction on public Wi-Fi. Even with an HTTPS connection, if a personal VPN application is not in use, then avoid these types of transactions.

Keep software updated. Regularly update your device's operating system and apps to defend against the latest security threats.

Disable automatic connection to Wi-Fi networks. This prevents devices from automatically joining potentially unsafe networks.

Use two-factor authentication (2FA). As already discussed, 2FA adds an extra layer of security, making it harder for attackers to gain access to any accounts—even if they have access to passwords.

Turn off file sharing. In a public setting, ensure file sharing is turned off to prevent unauthorized access.

Be wary of suspicious networks. Avoid connecting to networks with suspicious names or no password protection.

One thing many of my clients assume is that, even at five-star hotels, the networks are secure. That simply is not the case. Hackers make a lot of money; they can afford to stay at five-star hotels, too. To a good hacker, a high-end hotel Wi-Fi network is just another public Wi-Fi network.

Is Bluetooth Secure?

Bluetooth security is another area people wonder about, including whether to turn it off when not using it. The technology, widely used for wireless communication between devices, is generally secure—but it's not without its vulnerabilities. Here's an overview:

Encryption. Modern Bluetooth devices use encryption to protect data in transit. However, the level of security depends on the Bluetooth version and the device's implementation of it.

Vulnerabilities. Security researchers have identified various vulnerabilities in Bluetooth protocols. These include BlueBorne, Key Negotiation of Bluetooth (KNOB), and others that can allow unauthorized access or eavesdropping.

Security levels. Different Bluetooth applications offer varying security levels. For instance, a Bluetooth headset may have less rigorous security compared to a Bluetooth-enabled smart lock.

How to safely use Bluetooth:

Keep devices updated. Regularly update firmware and software. Manufacturers often release patches for known security issues. If Bluetooth has an auto-update feature, turn it on.

Pair devices in private. When pairing devices, do so in a private setting to avoid interception by unauthorized devices.

Use strong PINs. If a device requires a PIN for pairing, use a strong, unique one.

Turn off discoverable mode. Only keep a device in discoverable mode when needed to pair it with another device—then turn it off immediately afterward.

Be cautious with pairing requests. Don't accept pairing requests from unknown devices.

Use application-level security. For sensitive applications (like smart locks), ensure the app provides additional encryption or security measures.

Be aware of your surroundings. Avoid using Bluetooth in public areas where attackers might exploit vulnerabilities.

It's good practice to turn off Bluetooth when not in use, especially in crowded public areas and when not actively using it, to reduce the risk of eavesdropping or hacking attempts. This will also save battery power. But for many, the convenience of leaving Bluetooth on for fitness trackers, smartwatches, etc., outweighs the potential risks. Assess usage needs and risk tolerance.

To hack Bluetooth, a hacker does not necessarily need to be in very close proximity, but the risk is typically limited due to the nature of Bluetooth, a wireless technology designed for short-range communication. The range is usually within 10 meters (33 feet) for most devices, although some can reach up to 100 meters (328 feet) under ideal conditions.

In summary, while Bluetooth is relatively secure, it's important to be aware of its vulnerabilities and take proactive steps. Regular updates, cautious pairing, and mindful usage can significantly enhance Bluetooth security.

Conclusion

Public Wi-Fi networks, often found in places like cafes, airports, and hotels, are inherently less secure than private networks due to their open nature. They are a great working environment for hackers. Networks generally lack strong encryption, allowing for eavesdropping on internet activity, the theft of personal information, and potentially injecting malware onto devices.

To mitigate these risks, it's crucial to use cybersecurity protections like virtual private networks (VPNs) that encrypt internet connections, making it difficult for others to intercept data. Additionally, keep device software up to date, use firewalls, and avoid sensitive transactions like online banking when using public Wi-Fi. It's also advisable to connect to secure websites using HTTPS and to be wary of networks with suspicious names or those that don't require a password—these are often traps set by cybercriminals.

CHAPTER 9

Securing Cellphones

Cellphones have become a crucial extension of our daily lives. They are our primary means of communication, connecting us through calls, text messages, emails, and social media. While this constant connectivity keeps us in touch with family, friends, colleagues, and the world, the reality is if a phone falls into the wrong hands without adequate security, then much of your life will be in someone else's hands.

Smartphones provide instant access to vast amounts of information. And with features like calendars, reminders, alarms, and note-taking apps, cellphones function as personal assistants. GPS and mapping apps have transformed the way we navigate, making it easier to explore new places and get directions, but if a phone is not secured, these location services can also be exploited to track movements.

Mobile banking apps have made cellphones an integral part of many people's economic lives. So, your phone likely holds access to various online accounts, including financial, social media, email, and cloud storage.

Secure That Phone!

An unsecured phone can allow unauthorized access to your accounts, leading to potential privacy breaches and identity theft. What's more, mobile devices are susceptible to malware and viruses, just like computers.

Here are important tips to immediately protect your phone—and yourself:

LOCK-SCREEN SECURITY

Use the locking features on the phone. Use strong, unique passwords or biometric security (like fingerprint or facial recognition).

Passcode. Strong passcodes are critical. A mix of letters, numbers, and special characters or a longer numeric code are more secure than a simple four-digit code.

Pattern/swipe codes. Patterns or swipe codes are less secure than passcodes because they often leave smudge marks on the screen—which skilled hackers can interpret.

Biometrics. The best option is using facial recognition or a fingerprint. These add a strong layer of security that is hard to bypass. It's also the most convenient option.

A BETTER PHONE NAME
(NOT JUST YOUR NAME!)

Is your name being broadcast wherever you are? Might be. Most people never check to see what their phone is named—and oftentimes it's just their name, meaning the phone is transmitting that full name for everyone to see. If a hacker is nearby, they see the name, google it, find a picture, and then know exactly who they are dealing with—as in ready to steal from.

One of my clients was a very prestigious surgeon. As I was helping him secure his cell phone, we dealt with this issue. And I was quite surprised to see that his phone was named <Dr. Firstname Lastname>. That was not all. All his medical certifications were listed after his last name. I asked why he did this, and he said the IT team did it. That shocked me even more—they should know better. He said that when he goes to surgical centers, the hospital management knows he's there. I explained that they weren't the only ones—hackers would know too, making him a juicy target for a cyberattack.

Avoid using personally identifiable information when naming a phone. Choose a nondescript name to retain anonymity.

Renaming an iPhone or Android phone is a straightforward process. The process does change with different versions, but the ones listed below should still be close. Here's how to rename your phone:

iPHONES
- Open <Settings> app.
- Scroll down and tap <General>.
- Tap <About> (at the top of the list).
- Name the iPhone. Tap the first line, which shows the iPhone's name. Type in a new name that is not specific and does not identify you in any way. Tap <Done>.

ANDROID PHONES
- Swipe down from the top of the screen. Tap the <gear icon> or find the <Settings> app in the <app drawer>.
- Scroll down and tap <About phone> or <About device>.
- Find an option like <Device name>, <Phone name>, or <Edit> next to the current name.
- Tap the current name and enter a new somewhat innocuous name (not yours!).
- Tap <OK> or <Save> to confirm the new name.

Remember, changing the name of a device mostly

affects how it is identified by networks, Bluetooth, and connected devices.

CONFIGURE INSTALLED APPS

Keep a phone's operating system and apps updated with the latest security patches. Be cautious about downloaded apps and any permissions granted. iPhones and Androids both have an auto-update feature. Turn it on.

Permissions. Regularly review app permissions and disable any unnecessary ones, especially those relating to location, camera, or microphone access.

Dormant apps. Uninstall unused apps to minimize potential vulnerabilities.

Update. Keep apps updated to ensure they have the latest security patches.

ANTIVIRUS/ANTI-MALWARE SOFTWARE

I will discuss this in more detail in Chapter 10, but it is very important to have a reputable, commercial antivirus/anti-malware program installed and running on all mobile devices.

For example, I was working with a client who had recently ordered several things for his small business and was concerned because the shipment was late. He received a text message stating there was a problem and to click the link for more information. He wanted to know where his shipment was, so he clicked.

Unsurprisingly, he had fallen for a classic smishing attack, one designed specifically for mobile devices. Clicking opened a webpage that commenced uploading mobile-specific malware that took over his phone. After trying unsuccessfully for quite some time, we had to completely wipe his phone and reinstall the operating system.

Wondering if malware can infect a mobile device? The answer is absolutely yes. That's why having antivirus/anti-malware software running on a phone—all the time—is a must.

Tracking

Are you creating histories and maps of everywhere you go? Cellphones, by their very nature, are capable of tracking movements. Both Android and iOS use location services that are turned on by default. Here is how to disable unnecessary services.

iPHONES

Apple's Significant Locations feature is part of its broader location services. It tracks the past 90 days of movement and stores this data. If a hacker gets your iPhone, they can access it and build a map of daily movements—where you live, where you work, your kid's schools, and so on. Users concerned about privacy can disable the Significant Locations feature in their device settings.

- Tap the <Settings> app.
- Tap <Privacy & Security>.
- Tap <Location Services>.
- Tap <System Services>.
- Tap <Significant Locations>. Turn the feature to the off position. You can also click on the <Delete History> (in blue at the bottom).

ANDROID DEVICES

Google also tracks location and other data. Unless the privacy settings are changed, Google stores all of it on its servers—starting from when you first logged into a Google account (which was probably day one). This could cover years. As with the iPhone, you do not want hackers to gain access to this information.

To disable Location Tracking and manage privacy settings (including seeing what data Google has been collecting), visit Google account settings on an Android device or through a web browser (preferably Google Chrome).

- Log into your Google Account.
- Click the <Account Circle> (the one with your picture) in the upper right corner of the screen.
- Click <Manage Your Google Account>.
- Click <Data & Privacy>.
- Scroll down and click <Location History>.

- In the <Activity Controls> click <Turn Off Lo-cation History>. History can also be viewed and/or deleted.

Backups

Regularly back up a phone. Apple and Google both have backup features using iCloud and Google Drive, respectively. Here's how to back up each.

iPHONES
Using iCloud:
- Connect to Wi-Fi.
- Go to <Settings> → [your name] → <iCloud> → <iCloud Backup>.
- Turn on <iCloud Backup> (make sure you are logged in with your Apple ID).
- Tap <Back Up Now> (stay connected to Wi-Fi until the process is completed).

To check the backup:
- Go to <Settings>.
- Tap on your <Apple ID>.
- Select <iCloud> → <iCloud Storage> or <Manage Storage> → select your device.

Using a computer:
- Connect iPhone to a computer with iTunes (or Finder on macOS Catalina or later).

- Follow the on-screen steps to enter your device's passcode or to trust the computer.
- Select your iPhone when it appears in iTunes or Finder.
- Click <Back Up Now>.

Once the process is completed, see if the backup finished successfully in iTunes/Finder by checking the latest backup date and time.

ANDROID

Using Google Drive:

- Go to <Settings> on an Android device.
- Look for <System> → <Backup> (or <Backup and Reset> on some devices).
- Turn on <Backup to Google Drive>.
- Make sure you are connected to Wi-Fi.
- Tap <Backup Now> to protect data like apps, photos, contacts, and calendar events.

Using a computer:

- Connect an Android device to a computer via USB.
- If prompted, choose to transfer files or use the device as a media device.
- Files like photos, videos, and documents can be manually copied to the computer.
- A full backup might require third-party software or Android developer tools because Android does not offer a native full-

backup-to-PC feature like iPhones.

Remember, the specific steps might vary slightly based on the model and the OS version of the device. Always ensure that the smartphone has sufficient battery life before starting the backup process, or plug it into its charger.

iCloud/Google Account Security

Make sure to secure the linked iCloud or Google account with a strong password and 2FA.

REMOTE WIPE CAPABILITIES

This is a security feature that allows erasing a phone remotely in case it gets lost or stolen. This feature is crucial for protecting sensitive information and preventing unauthorized access to personal data, emails, contacts, photos, and other private files. Here's how it works generally:

Setup. Activate the remote wipe feature on the device. This is usually part of a larger suite of security tools provided by the operating system, like Find My iPhone for iOS or Find My Device for Android.

Activation. If the phone is lost or stolen, initiate the remote wipe through a web-based interface on a computer or other device. This requires logging into the account associated with the phone, like your Apple ID or Google account.

Execution. Once activated, the command is sent to the phone and the process begins. The phone will be restored to its factory settings, erasing all personal data.

Confirmation. Some systems will send a confirmation message that the wipe has been completed.

It's important to note a few things:

Internet connection. The phone needs to be connected to the internet for the remote wipe command to work.

Make sure you want to do this. Once the phone is erased, it's typically irreversible, so this feature should be used only in situations where you're certain the phone cannot be recovered.

Still trackable. In some cases, the phone can still be tracked even after a remote wipe, depending on the system and settings.

AUTO WIPE AFTER FAILED LOGINS

Many smartphones also have a security feature that triggers an auto wipe after a certain number of failed login attempts. This feature is designed to defend sensitive data in case the phone is lost or stolen. The specifics, such as the number of allowed attempts and whether this feature is enabled by default or needs to be manually activated, can vary depending on the phone's make and model and its operating system:

iPhones. Apple's iOS has a feature that, if enabled, will erase all data on the device after 10 consecutive incorrect passcode attempts. This feature is not enabled by default and must be turned on in the settings. It is recommended to turn this feature on.

Androids. The auto wipe feature on Android devices can vary more than iPhones, depending on the manufacturer and phone version. Some Android phones offer a feature that's similar to iOS, which wipes the device after a certain number of failed attempts. But it is not available on all models or versions.

It's important to note that while this feature can provide an extra layer of security, it also poses a risk. Passcodes can be forgotten, and children may make repeated incorrect attempts to unlock the phone.

Always ensure there is a backup of important data. Enabling remote wipe is highly recommended, especially if sensitive information is stored on your phone or it is used for business. It's a critical tool for protecting personal data and privacy in the event a phone is lost or stolen. However, always remember that this should be a last resort. Regular backups are important to ensure you don't lose anything important permanently.

iPHONE DELAY FEATURE

There is also a delay feature on iPhones that increases in duration with each successive failed passcode attempt:

1st to 5th attempts. No delay. If the wrong passcode is entered up to five times in a row, the iPhone does not impose any delay and allows another attempt immediately.

6th attempt. 1-minute delay.

7th attempt. 5-minute delay.

8th attempt. 15-minute delay.

9th attempt. 1-hour delay.

10th attempt. Depending on your settings, the tenth failed attempt can lead to either another 1-hour delay or a complete wipe of all data if the <Erase Data> feature is enabled.

It's important to note that these security measures are in place as a safeguard. If locked out of an iPhone, it's crucial to wait for the delay period to pass before trying again. Continuously entering the wrong passcode can result in longer delays and potential data loss, especially if the <Erase Data> feature is active.

APPLICATION PERMISSIONS

Securing applications on phones is important for several reasons. Many apps have access to personal data—contacts, photos, locations, and more—and if these apps are not secure, then that data isn't either.

Some apps may request permissions that are not necessary for their function. This overreach can lead to privacy concerns since the app may collect more than it needs, usually for purposes like targeted advertising or data selling.

Steps that can be taken to secure these apps include:

Setting app permissions. Regularly review and manage permissions and only grant those that are essential for the app's functionality. For example, a weather app might need access to your location, but a note-taking app probably doesn't.

Location information. Generally, there are four options: Never, Ask Next Time, While Using the App, or Always. Weather and map apps might be Always, but the majority of apps should be set to While Using the App.

Install reliable apps. Only download apps from trusted sources like the Google Play Store or Apple's App Store. These platforms have security measures to filter out malicious apps—though even that is not a guarantee, with many malicious apps having slipped through the Google and Apple filters. Avoid downloading apps from third-party sources. This is another reason why having antivirus/anti-malware software on mobile devices is very important.

Awareness of app behavior. Be aware of how apps behave. If one is requesting access to data or functionalities that don't seem necessary, it might be a red flag.

Mobile Device Takeover

Earlier I mentioned how cybercriminals can intercept those six- or eight-digit SMS text codes that are sent to smartphones. This is done via a mobile device takeover attack, which is an unauthorized party gaining control of a mobile device without the owner's consent. Understanding how this works and how to protect devices and accounts is crucial. Let's discuss the two most common attacks:

The easy way. The most common way is hackers already have your name and phone number. They determine the mobile service provider, go to the company's website, enter your phone number, and then try to hack the password.

The more sophisticated way. The other form of attack utilizes large databases on the Dark Web containing information obtained from previous cyber breaches.

Hackers query your name or phone number. If they find it, they will use any associated passwords as their starting point. Automated password cracking tools will first use an old password to see if it still works, then move onto a technique called fuzzing that makes minor changes to the password. This can work because hackers know people might only add an extra "!" or change the last character of the password from 5 to 6.

Either way, if successful, cybercriminals go into the management console and turn on call forwarding and text message forwarding. Now all calls and text messages go directly to them. You might not even realize this at first. Maybe you are busy working and don't notice the lack of calls or texts. Heck, maybe you're even kind of happy about it.

And now, even with two-factor authentication turned on, when the hackers try to get into an account, the SMS verification code goes to them. They login.

Let's say that you're using a password manager application, or have a 16-character complex password, and the hackers are now unable to get into the online mobile service account. The next attack method they try will be a social engineering attack.

Another mode of attack is a hacker going to the local phone store and using social engineering. They will have fake documentation, like a bogus driver's license and a few counterfeit utility bills, maybe even manufactured pay stubs. All they need to do is convince the person in the store that they are you when they share a tale of woe about losing their phone and needing to transfer the line to an old backup phone they have. If they're convincing enough, the busy retail worker—trying to be a nice person—transfers the line to their phone, which is called **porting** a phone line from one device to another. Now all calls and text messages are going to their phone.

That's not the worst part. If they are successful in using any of these attack methods, the next thing they do is visit online bank accounts. They won't try to hack bank passwords, knowing most people use two-factor authentication. Instead, they will do a password reset on bank accounts and hope that the one-time password gets texted to your number, which is now going (ported) to them. They reset passwords, then log into accounts. They try a small wire transfer to their bank. If it goes through, they've established their bank account as one that you send money to. Now they can start sending big wire transfers, draining accounts as much as they can before being noticed.

Preventive Measures

There are several ways to protect both the mobile service provider account and the phone itself. Let's start with the online account:

Two-factor authentication. As I've already said, turn on two-factor authentication for any online mobile service account.

Passwords. The second thing is creating strong complex passwords or having a password manager.

Account manager. The third is establishing an account manager for the mobile account.

Unique PIN. Finally, establish a unique verbal PIN or passcode for the account. Do not use the last four numbers of your Social Security number or date of birth, anything that is easy for hackers to guess. Make sure it is something unique but something easy to remember.

Having a unique verbal PIN or passcode should stop the social engineering method of attack. While the hackers may have all the fake documentation to try and convince the person in the store that they are you, they will not know the verbal PIN—and hopefully, the person in the store will not process the request.

If service is ever gone for five or ten minutes in an area where normally there is very good service, especially if people nearby with the same provider have four or five bars, then get in contact with the mobile service provider as soon as possible. Ask if they have made any changes to your account. If changes have occurred that weren't authorized, tell them they must deal with this right away.

Conclusion

By following the above steps, you can significantly reduce the risk of mobile device takeover and defend both the physical device and associated online accounts. Remember, mobile devices are an extension of your life. They are miniature computers that have access to sensitive personal information. Take the time and go through all the steps outlined in this chapter to make sure that devices are properly secured.

Properly configuring and securing mobile devices is crucial due to their integral role in our lives. Strong security measures, like using complex passwords, enabling two-factor authentication, using antivirus/anti-malware software, regularly updating software, and being cautious with app permissions all help safeguard data.

In an era when remote work is common, securing mobile devices also protects workplace intelligence and maintains the integrity of professional communications. Neglecting mobile device security can have far-reaching consequences, both personally and professionally.

If you have been a victim of a mobile device takeover, contact all your banks right away. They will go through all the most recent transactions to verify whether there have been any unusual activities.

CHAPTER 10

Antivirus and Anti-Malware Software

Hackers are making billions of dollars a day breaking into systems that are not secure. The necessity of antivirus or anti-malware software is paramount. They protect devices from a variety of malware, including viruses, worms, Trojan horses, ransomware, spyware, and adware. Each of these can harm systems in different ways, from stealing sensitive information to rendering your computer inoperable.

While similar in purpose, antivirus and anti-malware software differ in scope and the types of threats they combat.

How They Differ

Antivirus software traditionally defends against viruses—specific types of malicious software that replicate by attaching themselves to other programs. Antivirus programs typically focus on older, more established threats like viruses, worms, and Trojan horses. Detection is often signature based, which involves searching for known data patterns within executable code. However, many modern antivirus programs also include some behavioral-based detection to identify unknown viruses. Regular updates are crucial for antivirus software to be effective against new threats.

Anti-malware software, also known as anti-spyware, combats more advanced threats like spyware, adware, and potentially unwanted programs. It is more focused on newer, more sophisticated threats that may not be recognized by traditional antivirus software, including threats like ransomware, zero-day attacks[15],

---

[15] A zero-day attack refers to a cyberattack that exploits a previously unknown vulnerability in software or hardware. This means that the vulnerability is not yet known to the software or hardware vendor, and consequently, there is no patch or solution available to fix it at the time of the attack. The term "zero-day" refers to the fact that the developers have "zero days" to fix the issue because it has already been exploited by the time it is discovered. These attacks can be particularly dangerous because they can go undetected for a long time, giving attackers a window of opportunity to inflict damage or steal data without being noticed.

and sophisticated malware variants. Anti-malware software often uses behavioral-based detection, which monitors program behavior for suspicious activities, and heuristic analysis to identify new, unknown threats. Anti-malware tools also require regular updates but may be more focused on emerging threats and new malware techniques.

In recent years, the distinction between antivirus/anti-malware software has blurred. Many antivirus products now offer defenses against a wider range of threats, including those traditionally targeted by anti-malware. Likewise, these tools often include features to combat classic viruses and Trojan horses.

SAFEGUARDS THEY OFFER

For the best protection, use both types of software because they complement each other's strengths and provide a more comprehensive defense against a broader range of threats. However, it's important to ensure that they are compatible and don't interfere with each other. You will find that most well-known, reputable providers offer products that have antivirus/anti-malware features combined into a single product to provide the following safeguards:

Real-time security. This means they constantly scan systems for potential threats, preventing malware from taking root before it can cause damage.

Safe internet browsing. Integration with your internet browsers, including features that warn about unsafe websites or downloads, reduces the risk of unknowingly downloading malicious software.

Data protection. Malware can steal, corrupt, or delete data. Antivirus software helps safeguard personal information, financial material, and important documents from such threats.

System performance. Some forms of malware can significantly slow down computers and/or networks. By removing it, antivirus software can help maintain optimal system performance.

Prevent identity theft. By blocking spyware and other forms of malware, antivirus software helps in preventing identity theft.

Network protection. Antivirus software is essential for defending the network from being accessed by unauthorized individuals through malware.

Email protection. Email scanning features that can detect and block malicious attachments and phishing attempts.

Confidence in digital security. Having reliable antivirus defenses provides peace of mind and knowledge that your digital environment is being monitored for threats.

Here are three key points about antivirus/anti-malware software and how to get the most out of it:

1. It must be installed on all your devices. Not just laptops and workstations, but also cellphones and tablets, including all Apple products.

2. Make sure the auto-update feature is turned on. There are thousands upon thousands of new viruses and malware coming out every day, and the antivirus providers are updating their products almost daily[16]

3. Purchase an annual subscription from a reputable provider. Some even have family plans. Free antivirus software can miss many viruses or malware.

Conclusion

Antivirus/anti-malware software plays a crucial role in shielding computers and networks from a wide range of threats, including viruses, worms, Trojan horses, ransomware, and other forms of malicious software designed to steal data, damage systems, or disrupt operations. These programs offer real-time

[16] "Malware," AV-TEST, n.d., accessed January 9, 2024. https://www.av-test.org/en/statistics/malware/.

protection by constantly scanning for known threats and behaviors that are indicative of new, unidentified threats. By regularly updating their databases with the latest threat intelligence, these software solutions help protect against both known and emerging threats and thereby safeguard sensitive information, maintain system integrity, and ensure continuity of operations.

CHAPTER 11

Challenges and Opportunities of Social Media

Hackers love social media. When preparing a cyberattack, they will always go to social media sites to gather as much data about targets as possible. This might be an individual, a family, or a business. And it's not only cybercriminals that we have to worry about stalking us on social media. Common criminals also use social media sites to find out when families are on vacation and away from home for days or weeks. Stalking is also another kind of worry for many people, especially women.

Social media profiles often contain a wealth of personal information that can be exploited by hackers for identity theft, scams, or social engineering attacks.

Children especially may not understand the implications of sharing personal facts and how it can lead to privacy issues or unwanted contact. Social media can be a platform for cyberbullying, which can have significant emotional impacts, especially on children.

Hackers often use social media to trick people into revealing sensitive data or downloading malware through phishing or direct messages that contain malicious attachments or links. And what you—and your children—post online can have long-term effects, impacting future job prospects or college admissions.

Here is an example of how hackers use social media posts.

One of my clients, a couple, was taking their children on a summer vacation. They are at the airport and boarding the plane. The youngest son took a step back and snapped a picture—his mother, father, and two brothers—and because he was very excited, he posted the picture to his Facebook page with a comment saying something like "Off to Paris with the family. See you in a couple of weeks." His Facebook page and all his social media sites, including his brothers, were wide open to the world. No security whatsoever, using his real name for his profile.

What none of them knew was that they were being targeted. One thing cybercriminals do is set up fake persona profiles on different social media sites and then friend, follow, or connect with their targets. In this case, the hackers were friends with all three sons.

They also got excited when they saw the son's post and immediately created a spoofed email[17] to the head of finance and accounting of the father's business saying something like, "Hey Bob, we're boarding the plane now. I need you to send $50,000 to [name of vendor they did a lot of business with]." They added "thanks" at the end.

Normally their business had a good dual approval process for all outgoing payments, and for larger payments like this, the head of finance would review it with the father. But since he thought the email had come from the father, that box was checked. The head of finance knew they were on a plane heading to Europe and that the father could not get on a phone call for six or seven hours, by which time the banks would be closed. He wanted to get the payment out right away, so he sent the wire.

Unfortunately, the payment went straight to the cybercriminal's bank account. These guys were very good. Within a very short time after the money arrived, they turned it around, sent it offshore, and converted it into cryptocurrency. The family business had lost $50,000 because a kid posted a picture and a note on social media.

---

[17] Spoofing is a technique that hackers use to change the <from> address to make it look like whoever they want.

Most Popular Social Media Platforms

As of this writing, the most popular social media apps in the United States show a diverse range of platforms catering to various user preferences and needs. Each has its own privacy and security settings. The leading platforms are:

Facebook. Dominating the social media landscape, Facebook is used by 69 percent of adults in the United States. It's the top choice for staying connected with friends and family, following news, and participating in group discussions.

Instagram. Standing second with 40 percent of US adults using it. Known for visual storytelling through photos and videos, it attracts influencers, artists, and brands.

Twitter (now X). Used by 23 percent of US adults, offering a platform for real-time engagement, news updates, and public conversations. It's particularly noted for its influence in professional networks.

TikTok. Popular with 21 percent of the population, it makes a significant impact with its short-form video content that appeals mainly to young adults.

LinkedIn. Not really a social media site, though it is a significant platform, particularly for professional networking and job searching. In terms of overall presence, about 28 percent of the US population has a LinkedIn account.[18]

These platforms, each with their unique features and user base, continue to shape the digital landscape and social media trends. They also are the key sites where hackers go to gather data on potential targets.

Regularly review and adjust privacy settings on all social media platforms to limit who can see posts. Other than LinkedIn, there's no need to use your real name. Friends and family will know. Don't make it easy for hackers.

Teach children about the risks of sharing personal information, such as home addresses, phone numbers, and school locations. Teach children to be cautious about accepting friend requests or messages from strangers. Hackers and cyberbullies often use fake personas to get close to someone. Teach everyone to report any suspicious or uncomfortable experiences they encounter online.

Never post anything potentially problematic or allow friends to tag family members in a questionable picture or notification. Teach them to think before

---

[18] Shradha Dinesh and Meltem Odabaş, "8 Facts About Americans and Twitter as It Rebrands to X," Pew Research Center, July 26, 2023. https://www.pewresearch.org/short-reads/2023/07/26/8-facts-about-americans-and-twitter-as-it-rebrands-to-x/.

they post—once they do, it's out there forever, sometimes even if they delete it a minute later. A dubious post can come back to haunt them years later.

Use strong, unique passwords—as described earlier—for each social media account. Also, consider using a password manager. Enable 2FA on all accounts to add an extra layer of security. Social media accounts are one of the most frequently hacked parts of the internet. It is very difficult to regain control over an account once it has been hacked.

Security Steps for Various Platforms

To enhance the privacy and security settings on social media, follow these steps:

FACEBOOK

Rename your profile. Make it difficult for hackers to find you on social media. Go to <Account Center> → <Settings & Privacy> → <Settings> → <Personal Details> → <Profiles> → <Your Profile> → <Name>.

Check your public profile. View your profile in public mode to understand what information is visible to people who aren't friends.

Limit past permissions for posts. This restricts the visibility of your past posts. Go to <Settings & Privacy>

→ <Privacy Checkup> → <Who Can See What You Share> → <Continue> → <Next> → <Limit Past Posts>

Change permissions for future posts. Control who can see future posts and profile information. <Settings & Privacy> → <Privacy Checkup> → <Who Can See What You Share> → <Next> → <Default Audience>.

Change Facebook profile searchability. Adjust how others can find you on Facebook. This includes friend request settings, search visibility via phone number or email, and whether search engines can index your profile. <Settings & Privacy> → <Privacy Checkup> → <How People Can Find You on Facebook>.

Control off-Facebook activity. Manage data that third-party websites share with Facebook. <Settings & Privacy> → <Settings> → <Your Facebook Information> → <Off-Facebook Activity>.

Limit Facebook ad tracking. Adjust ad preferences to control how much of your data is used for targeted advertising. <Settings & Privacy> → <Privacy Checkup> → <Your Ad Preferences on Facebook>.

Turn off Facebook mobile location history. Prevent Facebook from tracking your precise location through the mobile app. Controlled through your mobile device. <Settings & Privacy> → <Facebook> →

<Location> → <Never>.

Remember, these settings are subject to change and may vary slightly depending on device and app updates, so it's a good idea to regularly review your privacy settings.

INSTAGRAM

Make the account private. Prevent non-followers from viewing your posts and stories. <Settings> → <Privacy> → <Private Account>.

Hide activity status. Conceal when you're online with <Privacy settings>.

Update story settings. Control who sees and interacts with your stories. <Privacy settings> → <Story>.

Enable two-factor authentication. Add an extra layer of security. <Settings> → <Security> → <Two-factor authentication>.

Remove location access. Block Instagram from accessing your device location through your phone's <Security> and <Privacy settings>.

Disable non-essential cookies. Limit data collection by adjusting cookie settings. <Settings> → <Privacy> → <Data permissions> → <Cookies>.

Change ad preferences. Adjust ad topics. <Settings> → <Ads> → <Ad Preferences> → <Ad topics>.

Block or restrict accounts. Manage interactions with specific accounts in their profile settings.

Modify interaction settings. Control who can message, mention, or comment on posts. <Privacy settings> → <Interactions>.

Don't sync contacts. Prevent contact syncing. <Settings> → <Contacts Syncing>.

Review Instagram data. Request a copy of your Instagram data. <Profile> → <Your Activity> → <Download your information>.

Clear browsing data. Delete Instagram browsing history. <Settings> → <Browser>.

FACEBOOK MESSENGER

Message delivery settings. Customize who can send messages directly to your inbox. <Profile picture> → <Privacy> → <Message Delivery>.

Restrict accounts. Limit interactions with specific contacts without blocking them in the chat settings.

Security alerts. Enable security alerts for end-to-end encrypted chats. <Privacy> → <Security Alerts>.

Limit story audience. Control who can see Messenger stories in <Story settings>.

Hide active status. Choose who can see your active status in the <Active Status settings>.

Delete search history. Clear Messenger search history in the search bar settings.

TWITTER (NOW X)

Use a strong password. Create a strong and complex password or use a password manager.

Enable two-factor authentication (2FA). This is very important on all your accounts.

Protect your tweets. Consider setting your account to private. This will make tweets visible only to your followers. <Settings> → <Security and Privacy> → <Tweet> privacy → <Enable Protect My Tweets>.

Disable tweet location. Turn off the option to add location to tweets to hide your movements and location privacy. <Settings> → <Security and Privacy> → <Tweet location> → <Disable Add A Location To My

Tweets>.

Beware of phishing attempts. Stay vigilant—suspicious messages might appear to be from X but are actually from hackers.

Manage app permissions. Regularly check and manage third-party apps that have access to your account. <Settings> → <Apps> → Review, revoking access when necessary.

Keep apps updated. Ensure that all the apps on your device, especially those related to X, are updated regularly to avoid security vulnerabilities.

Log out after use. Always log out from your account, especially when accessing it on public or shared devices. This prevents unauthorized access to your account.

To access these settings on mobile devices, tap your profile picture or the three-bar menu and select <Settings and privacy>. On a computer, click <More> in the left-hand menu and choose <Settings and privacy>. Additionally, under <Account> settings, you can enable password reset protection, which requires additional information for password changes, as well as manages your discoverability by email and phone number. For privacy, you can control photo tagging options, set content filters, and customize notification preferences. Implementing these steps will significantly enhance the security and privacy of your account.

TIKTOK

Protection from hacking. Access security settings by tapping the <Me> icon → the three dots in the upper right corner → <Manage my account>.

Two-factor authentication. TikTok doesn't offer this but does have a <Log in with verification code> feature for added security.

Disable password saving. Deselect the <Save login info> option in <Manage my account>.

Configuring privacy. To access privacy settings, tap <Me> → the three dots → <Privacy and safety> → <Discoverability> → Enable <Private account>. This limits content visibility to approved subscribers only. Remove unwanted subscribers from your profile page if necessary. Ensure that no personal information is in your profile description.

Remove profile from recommendations. To avoid appearing in recommendations, turn off <Allow others to find me> in the privacy settings.

Manage comments. Set restrictions on who can post comments. Choose <Friends> or <Off> under <Who can post comments>. For specific videos, disable comments in <Privacy settings> under the video options. Use the <Comment filters> to enable automatic filtering of spam and offensive comments and set up a keyword filter.

Control duets and reactions. Limit who can create duets with or reactions to your videos in the settings under <Who can Duet with you> and <Who can React to your videos>. Choose <Friends> or <Off>. For specific videos, disable duet/react in the video's <Privacy settings>.

Private messages settings. Manage who can send you private messages by selecting <Friends> or <Off> under <Who can send you messages>.

Prevent video theft. Disable downloading of your videos by others. Go to settings and select <Allow download> to <Off> to restrict others from downloading your videos.

Manage notifications. Control notifications by going to <Push notifications> in the account settings. Deselect the events you don't wish to be notified about.

Blocking users. To block a user, open their profile →

the three-dots → <Block> and confirm.

Making individual videos private. For new videos, after uploading select <Who can view this video> on the Post screen and choose <Friends> or <Private>. For existing videos, open the video access <Privacy settings> and adjust the visibility.

Remember to regularly review and update these settings to maintain your desired level of privacy and security.

LINKEDIN

Securing a LinkedIn account involves several steps to ensure that personal and professional information remains safe.

Create a strong password. As always, create a strong, complex password or use a password manager application.

Enable two-factor authentication. Go to your LinkedIn settings. Look for the security section. Select the option for <Two-Factor Authentication>. You can choose to receive a code via SMS or use an authenticator app. This adds an extra layer of security.

Monitor account activity. Regularly check your

account for any unusual activity. LinkedIn provides a feature to see where and when your account has been accessed.

Manage privacy settings. Go to your privacy settings. Adjust who can see your connections, who can send you invitations, and how others see your profile and updates. Be cautious about what personal data you share in your profile.

Be wary of suspicious messages and connection requests. Do not click on suspicious links or attachments sent via LinkedIn messages. Be cautious about accepting connection requests from people you do not know.

Use a secure and private email address. The email linked to your LinkedIn should be secure and used mainly for professional purposes. Consider using an anonymous one just for this purpose.

Update your LinkedIn app and browser regularly. Ensure that you're using the latest version of the LinkedIn app and web browser. Updates often include security patches.

Be careful with third-party applications. Be selective about which third-party applications you allow to access your LinkedIn account. Regularly review and revoke access to apps you no longer use or trust.

Review your connections. Periodically review your connections to ensure you are connected only with people you trust.

Following these steps can greatly enhance the security of a LinkedIn account, safeguarding personal and professional information from unauthorized access. Remember, staying vigilant and proactive about security is key in the digital age.

A Note About Genealogy Sites

There are now numerous genealogy websites that have become increasingly popular for individuals interested in exploring their family history. Some of the best-known ones include Ancestry, MyHeritage, FamilySearch, and 23andMe. They offer a variety of services, including DNA testing, access to historical records, and tools for building family trees.

However, their rise has raised concerns regarding privacy and data security. Hackers can potentially use these sites to gather information about individuals. Here are some of the ways:

Data breaches. Like any online platform, genealogy sites are vulnerable. If a site's database is hacked, personal information, including potentially sensitive genetic data, can be accessed by unauthorized parties.

Phishing scams. Hackers might use what they find on

these sites to craft personalized attacks. By knowing more about a person's family history, they can create more convincing fake emails or messages to trick people.

Security questions. Hackers can find the answers to your security and password reset questions, such as your mother's maiden name, the places and dates of births, and other personal information that many sites use as security prompts.

Identity theft. Details like birth dates, names, and historical addresses can be pieced together to create identity theft profiles.

Surveillance and stalking. In more extreme cases, these sites could be used for surveillance or stalking since they often contain detailed family connections and sometimes even current contact information.

Some steps to remain protected:

Strong passwords. Create strong complex passwords or use a password manager application.

Two-factor authentication. If offered, turn on two-factor authentication to add an extra layer of security to the account.

Stay private. Make sure that your family tree is private. There is no need for it to be public. If you want to share it with someone else, there are ways to do this that are not such an open target.

Conclusion

Social media users need to be aware of the risks. Use strong passwords (unique to each site), enable two-factor authentication when available, and be cautious about the amount of personal information shared online. Additionally, reading and understanding the privacy policies of these websites can help users make informed decisions about what they are comfortable sharing.

Remember, while social media can be a great way to stay connected and informed, it's crucial to understand the risks and take proactive steps to safeguard against danger.

Securing social media accounts is crucial due to their extensive role in your personal and professional life. These platforms contain sensitive data that, if compromised, can lead to identity theft, financial loss, and damage to personal or professional reputation.

Hackers often target social media for data mining, spreading malware, or conducting phishing attacks. Additionally, unsecured accounts can be used to spread misinformation or malicious content, potentially impacting a large audience. Proper security measures defend against unauthorized access and mitigate risk. Staying vigilant about security settings and updates also helps in safeguarding against evolving cyber threats, which will ensure that personal and sensitive data remains protected in an increasingly digital world.

CHAPTER 12

Identity Theft

Identity theft is a type of fraud that occurs when someone steals personal information—name, Social Security number, credit card number, and more—to commit fraud or other crimes. It can lead to various issues like unauthorized financial transactions, damage to your credit score, and even legal trouble if a crime is committed under your identity.

In the United States, this crime has escalated significantly in recent years—with alarming statistics emerging. In 2024, nearly 1.4 million cases of identity theft were reported nationwide. This suggests that soon the country is on track to exceed 2 million identity theft complaints, a number far higher than any year on record, dating back to 2001.

Estimated losses due to identity theft in 2024 total around $23 billion. The median loss for each fraud victim is approximately $500. In 2023, there were over a million reports of identity theft. This comparison indicates a continued rise in identity theft incidents year over year.

Experts estimate there is a new victim of identity theft every 39 seconds. Approximately one in 10 people will be a victim of identity theft. Additionally, nearly 33 percent of Americans have faced some form of identity theft at some point in their lives, a rate nearly three times higher than in other countries.

Government documents and benefits fraud are at the top of the identity theft list. Losses to government imposter scams increased $171 million from 2023 to a total of $789 million in 2024. Credit card fraud is also a major type of identity theft.

A Global Threat

Identity theft remains a significant and prevalent issue worldwide. While specific statistics can vary by region, several key trends highlight the scope of the problem. The frequency of identity theft incidents globally has been rising, partly due to the increasing digitization of personal information and the proliferation of internet usage. This trend is exacerbated by the growing sophistication of cybercriminals.

No country is immune. It's a global issue, affecting millions of people. Identity thieves use a range of methods, from traditional means like stealing mail or dumpster diving to more advanced techniques involving cyberattacks, phishing, and hacking into databases.

The consequences of identity theft are significant, affecting not just individuals but businesses, too. Victims may face financial loss, damage to credit scores, and the complex process of restoring their reputation and credit. Businesses, on the other hand, can suffer from financial losses, legal consequences, and damage to their reputation.

Ways to Defend Yourself

CREDIT FREEZE

This is the absolute best protection against identity theft. A credit freeze, also known as a security freeze, means potential creditors cannot access your credit report, which will make it more difficult for identity thieves to open new accounts in your name.

This prevents a common repercussion of identity theft. After cyber thieves have gathered personal information, they often then apply for dozens of credit cards, department store accounts, or even a bank account. For such businesses to open an account, they must run a credit check. If a check shows that you have a very good credit rating, businesses will grant a much higher credit limit. Cybercriminals then take a cash advance and run. However, if credit is frozen, businesses can't run a credit check and they won't open an account. That's why this is one of the absolute best ways to avoid being the victim of identity theft.

To place a credit freeze, contact each of the three major credit bureaus (Equifax, Experian, and

TransUnion) individually. Contact all three agencies either online or by phone. They will go through the identification process and then have you establish a verbal PIN or passcode that can be used later to unfreeze the account, which can be done over the phone or online.

It's usually free to freeze and unfreeze credit. A freeze remains in place until you choose to remove it; the credit bureaus are governed by federal law, which provides a consistent, legally defined process.

Freezing the credit of children and elderly family members is also a good idea. Children can still use credit cards to build their credit rating, but no one can open a new account in their name with their Social Security number. Since the elderly typically are not likely to buy a new house or other major item, it's wise to freeze their credit as well.

When you need to open a new account, ask the institution which credit agency they use. Contact it and unfreeze your credit. They will identify you, ask for the verbal PIN, and then unfreeze the account immediately. The credit can be unfrozen for a limited period, after which it will automatically refreeze.

CREDIT LOCK

A credit lock also restricts access to your credit report, but it's generally easier to lock or unlock as needed, often using a mobile app or webpage. Locks are offered by credit bureaus and are sometimes part of a subscription with a monthly fee, depending on the provider and the level of service.

The main advantage of a credit lock is convenience—you can lock and unlock it instantly. Unlike credit freezes, credit locks are not governed by federal law, so the protections and processes vary more broadly by credit bureau and service provider.

Is a credit freeze or a credit lock better?

The choice between the two depends on specific needs. A credit freeze is generally considered more secure because of legal protections and less susceptibility to being bypassed or unlocked without your knowledge. If you require frequent access to the credit report or you need to allow others to see it, for instance, when shopping for a loan, a credit lock might be more convenient.

Remember, though these steps can significantly reduce risk, no method is foolproof. It's essential to stay vigilant and proactive to truly safeguard personal information.

MONITOR ACCOUNTS REGULARLY

It is a good practice to regularly check bank and credit card statements for any unauthorized transactions. This helps detect any fraudulent activities earlier.

There are several companies, including the three major credit reporting agencies, that offer credit monitoring programs. Most prefer annual subscriptions. In addition to monitoring your credit report, they will keep an eye on things like your Social Security number, driver's license number, and other personally identifiable data. They also do Dark Web monitoring and send alerts if they see any activity using your information. Some banks offer this type of service without charge.

Conclusion

Protecting against identity theft is crucial due to its severe and long-lasting consequences. It involves unauthorized access to personal information, such as Social Security numbers, bank account details, and credit card numbers, which can be used for fraudulent activities. Victims of identity theft often face financial losses, damage to credit scores, and the arduous task of restoring their reputation and financial standing. This can all take years.

Additionally, the emotional and psychological stress caused by identity theft can be significant. The pervasive nature of digital transactions and online data storage increases the risk of identity theft, making it more important than ever to employ robust security measures, monitor financial accounts, and be vigilant about defending personal information. By doing so, individuals significantly reduce the likelihood of becoming victims of potentially devastating identity theft.

CHAPTER 13

Cryptocurrency and Digital Assets

Cyber thieves are very interested in stealing cryptocurrency and digital assets. As the prices for cryptocurrencies like bitcoin and ether have surged in recent years, they've become attractive targets for cybercriminals. Given their anonymity or pseudonymity, it is easier for thieves to hide their tracks compared to the traditional banking system.

If you have invested in them, then securing cryptocurrency and digital assets is crucial. But their digital nature makes them susceptible to various forms of cyber threats like hacking, phishing, and other forms of cyberattacks. Once a cryptocurrency transaction is confirmed, it's nearly impossible to reverse. This means that if thieves manage to steal cryptocurrency, it's very difficult for the victims to get it back.

An Easy Digital Target

Being entirely digital, cryptocurrencies can be stolen remotely, often with sophisticated hacking techniques. This is way more appealing than physically robbing a bank, especially since many users and exchanges still don't have foolproof security measures in place. Anyone dealing with cryptocurrencies or digital assets should be very cautious and employ strong security measures to protect their assets. Here are some key strategies:

Use a hardware wallet. Hardware (also called cold) wallets, like Ledger or Trezor, are physical devices that store your private keys offline, making them immune to online hacking. They are considered one of the safest ways to store cryptocurrencies.

Enable two-factor authentication (2FA). For any online crypto wallet or exchange, always enable 2FA. This adds an extra layer of security beyond just a username and password.

Use strong and unique passwords. Create complex passwords that are unique to each cryptocurrency account. Avoid reusing passwords across different sites.

Keep software updated. Regularly update your wallet software, computer, and mobile device to protect against vulnerabilities and security threats.

Beware of cryptocurrency phishing attacks. Be cautious about emails and messages that ask for your crypto credentials or direct you to suspicious websites resembling your wallet or exchange. The emails might look very legitimate. The best practice is to close the email, open a browser, go directly to the website, and log in to look for the information.

Use a secure internet connection. Avoid using public Wi-Fi networks for cryptocurrency transactions. Use a secure, private, and trusted internet connection.

Regular backups. Regularly back up your wallet, preferably in multiple locations, like USB drives and paper wallets, to safeguard against data loss.

Be educated. Stay informed about the latest security threats in the crypto space and the best practices for protecting assets.

Use trusted exchanges and wallets. Stick to well-known and reputable cryptocurrency exchanges and wallets.

Consider multi-signature wallets. For additional security—especially for large sums—use multi-signature wallets that require multiple private keys to authorize transactions.

The FTX Scandal

In 2022, as the value of cryptocurrency declined and some exchanges folded, FTX—maybe you've heard of it—remained strong. But that was a mirage. In November 2022, FTX crashed. It was a significant scandal, one of the worst in the industry's history, revolving around the mismanagement and criminal activities of Sam Bankman-Fried, the company's founder.[19]

The main issue concerned the misuse of funds. FTX and its sister company, Alameda Research, were discovered to be misusing customer deposits. Basically, Alameda frequently borrowed money from FTX customer assets, which led to a severe liquidity crisis. There also was a lack of financial transparency. FTX did not maintain standard financial reporting procedures, like balance sheets showing an ability to cover liabilities. This lack of transparency contributed to the severity of the crisis.

When things first went sideways—at least in public—the competing cryptocurrency exchange, Binance, stepped in to purchase FTX. However, that

[19] Amanda Hetler, "FTX Scam Explained: Everything You Need to Know," Tech Target, November 6, 2023. https://www.techtarget.com/whatis/feature/FTX-scam-explained-Everything-you-need-to-know.

offer was retracted due to concerns about mishandled customer funds and an ongoing US investigation.

FTX's collapse began with a leaked balance sheet and was exacerbated by a significant drop in the value of its FTT tokens, which then led to mass customer withdrawals. Bankman-Fried was arrested, faced multiple fraud charges, including using funds for personal gain and speculative investments, and was then found guilty.[20]

The Crypto Sector After FTX

The scandal had a notable impact on the broader cryptocurrency market, unleashing a drop in overall demand and value, though some recovery was observed later in 2023. The collapse of FTX has spurred discussions and a movement toward stronger regulation of the cryptocurrency industry,[21] highlighting the need for more robust oversight to protect consumers and investors.

---

[20] Associated Press, "FTX Founder Sam Bankman-Fried Guilty On All Counts of Fraud after Historic Cryptocurrency Collapse," *Politico*, November 2, 2023. https://www.politico.com/news/2023/11/02/sam-bankman-fried-guilty-fraud-00125161.

[21] "The FTX Crypto Scandal: 'Same Old-School Fraud, Just with New Technology,'" dwf, April 24, 2023. https://dwfgroup.com/en/news-and-insights/insights/2023/4/the-ftx-crypto-scandal-same-old-school-fraud-just-with-new-technology.

What are the best ways to protect yourself against similar scenarios? Here are five tips:

1. **Due diligence.** Research and understand the credibility and financial health of any cryptocurrency exchange or investment platform before using it.
2. **Diversification.** Spread investments across different assets and platforms to mitigate the risk of a single point of failure.
3. **Stay informed.** Keep up to date with news and developments in the cryptocurrency world, especially regarding regulatory changes and the financial stability of key players.
4. **Use regulated exchanges.** Gravitate toward exchanges that are subject to regulatory oversight since this can offer more protection and transparency.
5. **Be aware of the risk.** Recognize that cryptocurrency investments are inherently risky and invest only what you can afford to lose.

Researching and finding reputable and safe cryptocurrency exchanges involves several steps.

Get educated. It's good practice to read reviews and user feedback on websites like Trustpilot and Reddit, which can provide user experiences and feedback on different exchanges. However, be cautious. Some reviews may be biased or fake. Don't rely on any single review. Join online forums and communities to learn about exchanges and engage with crypto communities on platforms (as of this writing) like BitcoinTalk, CryptoCompare, or specific subreddits. These communities often discuss and review different exchanges.

Tap into analysis. Use financial news and analysis websites like (as of this writing) CoinDesk and CoinTelegraph, which provide news and analysis on cryptocurrency exchanges and the broader market.

Find regulated exchanges. Check regulatory compliance by finding exchanges that are compliant with regulations in their operating countries. Compliance with regulations like Know Your Customer (KYC) and Anti-Money Laundering (AML) can be a good indicator of an exchange's legitimacy.

Examine security features. A reputable exchange should offer robust security features, such as two-factor authentication, encryption, and cold storage for funds. Check to see whether the exchange has a history of security breaches.

Know who's running things. Research the leadership team and the company background. A transparent exchange should provide knowledge about its founders and team members. A strong background in finance or technology is a positive sign.

Assess liquidity and trading volume. High liquidity and trading volume can indicate a healthy and active exchange. This information is usually available on the exchange's website or crypto market analysis sites.

Insurance and security audits. Some exchanges have insurance policies to protect users' funds against theft or other issues. Additionally, exchanges that undergo regular security audits by reputable firms are generally more trustworthy.

User interface and customer support. A user-friendly interface and responsive customer support are important, especially for beginners in crypto trading. Test the customer support response time and helpfulness.

The Range of Offered Cryptocurrencies and Fees. While a wide range of cryptocurrencies is advantageous, it should not be the sole criterion for selection. Also, understand the fee structure for trading, depositing, and withdrawing funds.

Geographic restrictions. Ensure that the exchange operates in your country and complies with local regulations.

Start small. Once you select an exchange, begin with small amounts to test its functionality and reliability.

Remember, the cryptocurrency space is evolving rapidly. Due diligence is essential. It's also advisable to diversify and not rely on a single exchange for all transactions. The FTX scandal serves as a stark reminder of the risks associated with the largely unregulated world of cryptocurrency, underscoring the importance of regulatory oversight and prudent investment practices.

Conclusion

Remember, the responsibility of securing digital assets lies primarily with the individual owner. There are not really any federal regulators backing up the system or providing recourse in case of theft or loss. So, it's important to be vigilant and proactive in employing security measures.

Protecting cryptocurrency and digital assets is difficult. Their very nature makes them vulnerable to unique risks such as hacking, fraud, and technical failures. Additionally, the anonymity and irreversible nature of blockchain transactions make it difficult to recover funds once they are lost or stolen.

The lack of a centralized authority places the responsibility of security entirely in the hands of the asset holder, necessitating strong personal security measures. Moreover, the increasing value and popularity of digital assets make them attractive targets for cybercriminals. Therefore, employing robust security practices like hardware wallets, two-factor authentication, updated software, and vigilance about phishing is essential for safeguarding these assets.

PART II

PROTECTING YOUR BUSINESS

CHAPTER 14

Small Businesses and Niche Industries Are Juicy Targets

Welcome to Part II of the book. Now I'll focus on safeguards for businesses. If you've read Part I, there will be some redundancies since we're dealing with the same threat actors and many of the same procedures to defend against them. But in Part II, I will discuss many things unique to protecting a business.

I will focus on small-to-midsize businesses (SMBs). If you manage a large business or are part of a big corporation, then see my sibling book Cybersecurity: Everything an Executive Needs to Know. In it, I focus on the cybersecurity responsibilities facing large corporations, specifically boards of directors and C-suite executives.

I've worked with many business owners, helping them better secure their businesses. I often hear things like, "We are a small business. Why would cybercriminals come after us?" or "We are in a niche industry. Why would hackers target us?" The reality is that cybercriminals will go after any size business. They don't care who they can steal money from. If it's easier to extort $10,000 or $20,000 from an SMB, they'll do it because that's just part of their business decision-making. Doing that to 50 or 100 SMBs can bring in a couple million dollars. As the saying goes, do it enough and pretty soon you're talking real money. Also, SMBs are often connected to much larger businesses and therefore can provide cybercriminals an access point into them.

One of the best examples of this scenario happened back in 2013. The Target department store chain suffered a cyber breach, and hackers ended up with 40 million credit card numbers and data on 70 million customer accounts. But the attack was not on Target directly. Instead, criminals attacked one of their vendors—a small mechanical services company in Pittsburgh that provided services to about 130 regional Target stores—did not have the proper cybersecurity in place. It suffered a cyber breach. After the cybercriminals got into this company's system, they quickly realized they had hit pay dirt. They acquired the login credentials and a connection into Target's network;

they chose not to steal anything from the vendor. Instead, they exploited the connection to Target. This is another reason why cybercriminals like to go after SMBs: they often have weaker cybersecurity protections. They're smaller fish that can be used to catch bigger ones.

Risks to Small-to-Midsize Businesses

Risks and threats to small-to-midsize businesses are a significant concern. These businesses often face unique challenges due to limited resources and expertise when compared to larger corporations. Here are some key points to consider:

Ransomware attacks. SMBs are increasingly targeted by ransomware attacks. Data is encrypted, rendering it inaccessible until a ransom is paid. These attacks can be devastating, leading to significant downtime and financial loss. (This will be covered in more detail in Chapter 16.)

Phishing scams. Employees at SMBs are often less trained to recognize phishing attempts, where fraudulent emails or messages trigger the theft of sensitive information. These scams can lead to financial losses. (Chapter 15 will cover these in more detail.)

Data breaches. SMBs often store sensitive customer and business material. A breach can occur due to weak cybersecurity practices. This can open the business up to fines and, in some cases, class-action lawsuits.

Inadequate backup and recovery plans. In the event of data loss due to cyberattacks, many SMBs may not have robust backup and recovery systems in place, making it difficult to restore operations quickly.

IoT vulnerabilities. With the increasing presence of Internet of Things (IoT) devices, SMBs are exposed to new vulnerabilities. These devices often lack strong security features and can be easy targets for cyber-criminals.

Insider threats. Whether intentional or accidental, employees can pose a significant risk. This includes mishandling data, using weak passwords, or falling prey to social engineering attacks.

Compliance risks. SMBs must comply with various regulations, like the General Protection Data Regulation (GDPR) and the Health Insurance Portability and Accountability Act (HIPAA). Noncompliance due to cyber incidents can lead to hefty fines and legal issues.

Supply chain attacks. SMBs can be compromised through their supply chain relationships when attackers target less-secure partners as an entry point.

Limited cybersecurity awareness. Often, SMBs do not prioritize cybersecurity due to a lack of awareness about the extent of threats and their potential impact.

To mitigate these risks, SMBs should invest in basic cybersecurity practices like regular software updates, employee training, secure backup systems, and consulting with cybersecurity experts. Additionally, cybersecurity insurance might be a prudent step to manage financial risks associated with cyber incidents.

Dealing With a Lack of Internal Resources

Many SMBs lack the resources to manage comprehensive cybersecurity measures, including both financial constraints and a lack of in-house expertise.

That's why IT and cybersecurity firms that specialize in providing services to SMBs are such an important resource:

Direct cybersecurity services. Managed service providers (MSPs) for IT and managed security service providers (MSSPs) for cybersecurity are companies that will manage threat prevention for SMBs (some MSPs do both). These firms understand the unique challenges and requirements that SMBs face, such as limited budgets and resources compared to larger enterprises.

Cybersecurity consultants. There are also firms

offering consulting in the form of a virtual CISO (Chief Information Security Officer) or CISO-as-a-service. These firms provide cybersecurity expertise and leadership to organizations on a flexible, often part-time basis. This is particularly valuable for businesses that either may not require or find it affordable to have a full-time, in-house CISO. And if you don't need the full services of an MSSP, virtual CISO firms are excellent resources for analyzing an organization and providing recommendations on how to better secure it.

When selecting an outside firm, an SMB should consider several key factors:

Expertise and experience. Look for a firm with proven expertise in IT and cybersecurity, preferably in the SMB sector. They should be familiar with the common challenges SMBs face and offer tailored solutions.

Services offered. Ensure the firm provides a range of services that meet your specific needs, including network security, data protection, cloud services, compliance assistance, and more. It's beneficial if they offer proactive monitoring and response services.

Security operations center. The better firms will have a 24/7 security operations center (SOC) that will monitor networks and devices at all times. Hackers never sleep or are on the other side of the world (their daytime is our nighttime). And they don't celebrate our holidays.

Reputation and references. Check the firm's background through client testimonials, case studies, or industry awards. It's helpful to ask for references or contact existing clients to get firsthand feedback.

Cost and flexibility. As SMBs often operate with limited budgets, it's important to find a firm that offers cost-effective solutions without compromising quality. They should be flexible in customizing services to fit specific budgets and needs.

Compliance and standards. The firm should be knowledgeable about the relevant latest industry standards and compliance requirements. This is crucial for maintaining data privacy and meeting regulatory obligations.

Customer support and communication. Good customer service and clear, consistent communication are vital. The firm should be responsive to queries and provide regular updates about IT and cybersecurity status.

Scalability. Choose a firm that can scale its services as a business grows. Your IT and cybersecurity needs will evolve, and the firm should be able to accommodate these changes.

Cybersecurity training. Since human error is a major factor in cybersecurity breaches, check that the firm offers training so employees can recognize and avoid potential threats.

Incident response plan. Ensure the firm has a robust cybersecurity incident response plan to quickly and effectively deal with any security breaches or IT issues.

Technology and tools. Evaluate the firm's technology and tools. They should employ up-to-date, advanced solutions to defend a business effectively.

Researching and selecting the right IT and cybersecurity firm is a crucial decision for an SMB. It's advisable to take the time to evaluate multiple firms to find the best fit for your specific needs and budget.

Who is attacking SMBs?

In Chapter 1, we discussed in detail three categories of cyber thieves—hacktivists, nation-states, and cybercriminals. The same groups attack SMBs. While nation-states might go after a business that is creating intellectual property, the group to be most concerned about is cybercriminals. As stated earlier, cybercrime is now the world's third-largest global economy after the economies of the United States and China. Cybercriminals are making an astronomical amount of money from cybercrime. There are estimates that cybercrime earnings will exceed $10 trillion by the year 2025.

Small and medium-size businesses are increasingly being targeted due to:

Limited resources. SMBs often have limited defenses against cybersecurity, making them more vulnerable to attack when compared to larger organizations with more robust security measures.

Premium data. SMBs oftentimes have access to customer information and intellectual property that are lucrative targets.

Business connections. SMBs are frequently part of larger supply chains and can serve as entry points to compromise bigger, more secure networks.

Conclusion

Small and medium size businesses must prioritize defending their operations due to the increasing prevalence and sophistication of cyber threats. By either bolstering their own cybersecurity practices or investing in a managed service provider (MSP), SMBs can effectively safeguard their data, customer information, and intellectual property. MSPs offer expertise, resources, and continuous monitoring that many SMBs lack internally. They can be a crucial investment to not only protect against financial losses and breaches but also to maintain customer trust and compliance with regulatory requirements. In today's landscape, cybersecurity is not just a technical necessity but a fundamental aspect of business resilience and reputation management.

This situation is compounded by the fact that many SMBs lack awareness or underestimate the risk, which leads to inadequate preparation and response strategies. As a result, SMBs become attractive targets for cybercriminals seeking easier access to valuable data or ways to exploit vulnerabilities for financial gain.

CHAPTER 15

Phishing

With so many very skilled hackers working 24 hours a day, what do you think is their primary method of attack? How are they getting into our business systems? A report by SANS Institute, the world's largest provider of cybersecurity training and certification, stated that 95 percent of all cyberattacks are a result of a successful phishing email.[22] I've already discussed this in Chapter 2, but I will now go into more detail about focused attacks on SMBs and some additional security measures that businesses should put in place.

Education and awareness are crucial steps that businesses can take immediately. Educate every employee about what phishing is, what to look for, and why it is so important to protect business operations by being cautious.

---

[22] Weinberg, "How to Blunt Spear Phishing Attacks."

New Tech, New Dangers

In the past, it was easy to spot a phishing email due to poor grammar and spelling mistakes. While those still exist, tools like the much-ballyhooed ChatGPT have made these scams look more legit. Using Artificial Intelligence (AI) tools to create dangerous emails is a significant concern. Hackers can leverage the tech in several ways to target businesses, like creating an email targeting businesses in specific sectors with text that makes it easy to just click on a link. And there are no errors in spelling or grammar, making the emails look perfectly normal. This is one reason why training is so important for all employees of a business.

Another tactic starting to arise is the Look-Alike-Domain attack. Hackers buy a domain name that is very similar to the one they want to impersonate. For example, if they want to impersonate the business domain www.mybusiness.com, the cybercriminals can purchase the domain <www.mybuslness.com> or <www.mybusiness.c0m>. Then, knowing that most people just glance at an email's <from> address, they track down the real name of a person at the real business. Employees see the real name of a person they're used to interacting with and don't pay attention to the slightly different domain name.

That's why it's important to look closely at the entire <from> address. If you have any doubt at all, hover

over it for a second or two, or even click on it, to see where the email actually originated.

Here is a real-world example: A business owner walked into his office and his assistant said, "Hey boss, I am working on that $50,000 wire transfer. It should go out shortly." Puzzled, the boss, responded, "What $50,000 wire?" His assistant replied, "The one you emailed me about this morning." Huh? He asked to see the email. When she pulled it up, they both saw that it appeared to come from him, his name was spelled correctly, and so it looked legit. Now he started thinking they had a cyber breach. But when they looked closer, they saw that there was a small misspelling of the domain name, with the letter <m> changed to <rn>. Aha, it was a breach. Luckily, that transfer wire was never sent.

Ways to Protect Businesses From Phishing

Provide regular training to employees. A comprehensive cybersecurity awareness program is crucial for businesses due to several key reasons:

Human factor mitigation. People are often the weakest cybersecurity link. Training helps employees recognize and avoid common threats like phishing, social engineering, and malware. Via consistent education efforts, businesses can significantly reduce the risk of breaches caused by human error.

Regulatory compliance. Many industries have strict data protection and privacy regulations. Training programs ensure that employees understand and comply with them, thereby avoiding legal and financial penalties.

Defending against evolving threats. Cyber threats are constantly advancing. Regular training helps employees stay updated on the latest threat landscape and cyber best practices.

Cultivating a security-first culture. Continuous training builds a culture of security within the organization. Employees become more vigilant and responsible about security in their daily activities.

Reduced risk of data breaches. Educated employees are less likely to fall victim to cyberattacks, which leads to lower risk. This safeguards the company's assets, reputation, and customer trust in them.

Cost savings. Expenses from a breach can be substantial. Investing in training is cost-effective compared to the financial impact associated with a breach, including remediation costs, fines, and lost business.

Customer confidence. Demonstrating a commitment to cybersecurity can enhance customer trust. People are naturally more likely to do business with companies that take security seriously.

Employee empowerment. Training empowers employees with knowledge and tools to defend themselves and the organization. This makes them an active part of the company's security defense.

A comprehensive cybersecurity awareness training program is essential for businesses to mitigate risks, comply with regulations, protect themselves against evolving threats, and maintain customer trust and confidence.

If contracted with an MSSP for IT and cybersecurity services, they should hopefully also provide cybersecurity awareness training for all employees. It is important to avoid one-and-done training. Comprehensive annual training is good, but periodic training and awareness throughout the year is also warranted.

If your MSSP does not provide this type of training, several third-party companies specialize in cybersecurity awareness training. Make sure to use a reputable provider that stays up to date on the latest cybersecurity attacks.

Email Filtering

Ideally, most phishing and spam emails can be filtered from employees' inboxes. Implement advanced email filtering and related security solutions. For businesses, this is crucial for several reasons. While filtering by providers like Microsoft or Gmail is beneficial, it may not be sufficient for business needs due to several factors:

Advanced threat protection. Email is a common vector for phishing, malware, and ransomware. While Microsoft and Gmail offer basic defenses, specialized inbound email filtering systems provide more advanced threat-detection capabilities using sophisticated algorithms and continuously updated threat intelligence that identifies and blocks new and evolving threats.

Customization and control. Businesses often have unique security needs and policies. Inbound email filtering offers greater customization and control, allowing businesses to tailor rules and thresholds according to their specific requirements. This helps to better align internal security policies with regulatory compliance requirements.

Reduced false positives and negatives. Effective email filtering minimizes false positives (legitimate emails marked as spam) and false negatives (spam emails getting through). Specialized filters offer more precision, reducing disruption to business communication and ensuring important emails are not missed.

Compliance and legal requirements. Some industries

have stringent regulatory expectations regarding data protection and privacy. By ensuring that sensitive information is properly handled, custom inbound email filtering, helps maintain compliance with laws like GDPR, HIPAA, and others.

Integration with other security systems. Inbound email filtering systems can integrate with a business's existing security infrastructure, like firewalls and intrusion detection systems, providing a more comprehensive security posture. This integration helps in better overall threat management and response.

Reporting and analytics. These systems often come with detailed capabilities that provide insights into the threats targeting the organization and the effectiveness of the email filters. This data is invaluable for refining security strategies.

User education and awareness. Advanced systems can be used to train and educate users about email threats, configured to flag potential phishing emails in a way that educates the recipient about identifying such threats.

Advanced warning. These systems can be configured to highlight potential issues. For example, they can add notices like <EXTERNAL> to email subject lines to alert an employee that a message is from outside of the company. The employee now knows to be more cautious with the message and any links or attachments.

Talk to your MSP or MSSP about setting up an inbound email filtering system for the business. While Microsoft and Gmail provide a good baseline of protection, the complexity and specificity of businesses often necessitate the use of dedicated systems. These offer enhanced security, customization, compliance support, and integration capabilities that are essential for robust business email security.

Conclusion

In summary, 95 percent of all cyberattacks are the result of successful phishing emails. It is very important to the long-term success of the business to implement proper cybersecurity defenses. Protecting a business against this mode of assault is crucial due to the severe consequences of successful attacks, which often include financial loss, data breaches, and damage to reputation.

Phishing exploits human vulnerabilities, which makes user education and awareness paramount. By training employees to recognize and appropriately respond to them, businesses can significantly reduce the risk of a successful attack.

Additionally, implementing technical measures like inbound email filtering systems provides an essential layer of defense. These systems can identify and block phishing emails before they reach users, thereby reducing the likelihood of human error. Combining user education with robust technical defenses creates a more secure environment, safeguarding the business's assets, data, and trustworthiness.

CHAPTER 16

Ransomware Can Cripple a Company

Chapter 3 discussed ransomware regarding families. This chapter is about how businesses can defend themselves against ransomware attacks, and if the worst happens, how to react to a successful attack.

Ransomware, which is on the rise, involves malicious software that encrypts the victim's files and the subsequent demand for a ransom to restore access. Reasons for the rapid growth of such attacks include their ease of deployment, the potential for high financial returns, and the growing sophistication of ransomware that exploits vulnerabilities in networks and systems.

Costs to victims include not just the ransom, but also the downtime, disruption, and potential reputational damages. Ransoms can range from a few hundred dollars for individuals to millions of dollars for large organizations. This represents substantial costs to the global economy that are passed onto consumers.

One prominent example is the May 2021 ransomware attack on Colonial Pipeline, one of the largest pipeline operators in the United States. Carried out by a cybercriminal group known as DarkSide, Colonial Pipeline's networks were infiltrated, ransomware deployed, and soon data was effectively encrypted. Not long after this, there was a demand for payment to restore access.

This event led to the shutdown of approximately 5,500 miles of pipeline transporting gasoline, diesel, and jet fuel across the eastern United States. The disruption caused widespread fuel shortages, panic buying, and an increase in gas prices. Colonial Pipeline reportedly paid a ransom of $4.4 million in bitcoin cryptocurrency to regain access to their systems. The attack underscored critical infrastructure's vulnerability to cyber threats and prompted increased governmental focus on enhancing cybersecurity measures in vital sectors.

The Perpetrators are Real Criminals

It's important to note that paying a ransom does not guarantee that data will be decrypted or that the attackers won't demand more money. Additionally, paying ransoms can encourage further criminal activity. For these reasons, many law enforcement agencies advise against paying ransoms. But that's easy for them to say. They're not locked out of their computers.

In some cases, hackers will play the two-ransom card. Once they get into a network, they then go looking for the most sensitive content—financials, legal records, personally identifiable data, customer lists, and so on. When they find some, they make a copy—sometimes even forwarding a screenshot to show which files and folders they've stolen. Then they encrypt the network. The second ransom results in either the return of the stolen information or a pledge to delete it once the ransom is paid. They've got you coming and going.

Organizations are advised to focus on preventive measures to mitigate the risk of ransomware attacks. It's the much cheaper option. There are several things that businesses need to be concerned about:

DATA ENCRYPTION

Ransomware typically encrypts the infected system, rendering it inaccessible. This can lead to the disruption of business operations. There have also been cases where the data could never be decrypted, and businesses had to completely rebuild their entire networks and systems.

FINANCIAL LOSS

Besides the ransom payment, businesses can suffer financial loss due to downtime, recovery efforts, and potential legal liability if sensitive data is exposed. According to the British-based security firm Sophos, the average cost of remediation for a 2024 ransomware attack in the United States was approximately $1.85 million.[23] This figure excludes ransom payments which average approximately $2,73 million in 2024.

It's notable that this cost has significantly increased from previous years. For instance, the average total cost of remediation more than doubled from $761,106 in 2019 to around $1.85 million in 2024. This trend indicates a substantial rise in the financial impact of ransomware attacks on organizations.

REPUTATION DAMAGE

A ransomware attack can damage a business's reputation, leading to a loss of customer trust and potentially long-term harm to the brand.

LEGAL AND COMPLIANCE RISKS

If the ransomware leads to a breach, especially involving personally identifiable information (PII) or other sensitive material, the business may face legal

---

[23] John Shier, "Ransomware Recovery Costs vs. the Ransom Demands," Sophos, n.d., accessed January 9, 2024. https://www.ft.com/partnercontent/sophos/ransomware-recovery-costs-vs-the-ransom-demands.html.

penalties and noncompliance issues under various data protection regulations.

CONTINUED VULNERABILITY
Paying the ransom does not guarantee that the hackers will follow through and return access. Also, it may mark the business as a target for future attacks.

Ways to Safeguard Against Ransomware

REGULAR BACKUPS
Maintain regular backups of critical data and ensure they are stored separately from the network, meaning not connected to it. This can help the systems/networks quickly recover from an attack. Ideally, you want two backups of everything. This could be in two separate cloud environments or one in the cloud and one at an off-site, off-network location.

For example, a few years ago, a business owner, who was a victim of a ransomware attack, thought he had a very good backup plan in place. Every Sunday night, he did a full backup of the company's entire network, then late each weeknight, he did an incremental backup of what had changed during that day. But when asked if he was able to do a full restore following a ransomware attack, his response was quite surprising. The data could not be restored because all his backups went to a server on the main network. So, the hackers got into the network, searched for and found his backup server, then encrypted it as well. He ended up having to pay the ransom. So, make sure backups are off-network.

UPDATE AND PATCH SYSTEMS

Keep all software and operating systems up-to-date with the latest patches. Many ransomware attacks exploit vulnerabilities before they have been patched. If you are using an MSSP, discuss with the provider how quickly they can update systems when a new patch becomes available. If the business is doing this internally with an in-house IT team, then have a patch management policy in place.

There are critical, high, medium, and low patches that come out almost every week. Microsoft releases patches on the second Tuesday of every month (Patch Tuesday). There could be 80 to 100 patches released each Patch Tuesday. The critical ones must be done immediately. The high ones need to be completed within a relatively short period (one or two weeks). Many businesses never get to the medium and low patches because there are so many critical and high ones to patch right away.

EMPLOYEE TRAINING

As previously mentioned, educate employees about the risks of ransomware and best practices for cybersecurity, such as not clicking on suspicious links and not downloading unverified attachments.

ANTIVIRUS AND ANTI-MALWARE SOLUTIONS

Implement robust antivirus and anti-malware solutions to detect and prevent ransomware infections. This will be discussed in Chapter 23.

NETWORK SEGMENTATION

Network segmentation is a crucial defensive strategy against ransomware attacks that involves dividing a network into smaller, distinct segments or subnetworks, each of which operates independently. This approach limits the spread of ransomware via containment within a single segment, thereby reducing its impact across the entire network. Segmentation also makes it more difficult for attackers to move laterally within a network because they must overcome additional barriers to access different segments. Additionally, network segmentation allows for more effective monitoring and management of network traffic since administrators can more easily identify and respond to suspicious activities within individual segments.

By implementing such a structure, organizations can significantly enhance their resilience against ransomware attacks, ensuring that even if one segment is compromised, the rest of the network remains protected. This method is particularly effective in large organizations with complex network structures, where the potential impact of ransomware can be extensive.

ACCESS CONTROLS

Implement strict access controls and the principle of least privilege. Limit administrative privileges and ensure employees have access only to the data they need for their tasks. Access controls are a crucial defense mechanism against ransomware attacks. By regulating who can access specific resources in a network, potential ransomware damage can be curtailed.

The principle of least privilege is fundamental to this approach, ensuring that users have only the minimum level of access necessary. This minimizes the risk of ransomware spreading across the network when a user's account is compromised. Effective access control strategies often include a combination of user authentication, role-based access control, and regular audits of access rights to ensure they remain appropriate. By reducing the number of people who have access to critical systems and data, the potential impact of ransomware is significantly mitigated, making it a less attractive target for attackers.

INCIDENT RESPONSE PLAN

Having an incident response plan is crucial. Such a plan outlines proactive measures and reactive strategies to minimize damage and recover from an attack. Key components include the identification of critical assets, regular backups, staff training, and establishing communication protocols for a coordinated response. The plan should also detail steps for isolating infected systems, eradicating the ransomware, and restoring systems from backups.

Regularly updating and testing the plan ensures preparedness for evolving ransomware tactics. Additionally, involving law enforcement and cybersecurity experts can provide valuable support and expertise in managing an incident and preventing future attacks. This comprehensive approach not only mitigates the impact of ransomware but also enhances overall cybersecurity resilience.

CYBER INSURANCE

Cyber insurance has emerged as a vital defensive strategy against ransomware attacks. It provides financial protection for businesses and individuals, which helps to mitigate the costs associated with data recovery, business interruption, legal fees, and other expenses. By transferring some of the financial risks to an insurance provider, policyholders can alleviate the immediate financial strain of a cyberattack. Moreover, cyber insurance policies often include support services, such as access to cybersecurity experts who can assist in managing and recovering from an attack.

However, it's crucial to note that cyber insurance is not a replacement for robust cybersecurity measures. It should be part of a comprehensive risk management approach that includes strong security practices and employee training to prevent ransomware attacks in the first place. Cyber insurance can be a crucial asset for businesses, especially in an era when cyber threats are increasingly common and sophisticated. Here are some points to consider about the necessity and difficulty of obtaining cyber insurance:

Protection against the impact of an attack. Cyber insurance provides a financial backstop against various forms of cyber threats, such as data breaches, ransomware attacks, and other forms of cybercrime.

Business continuity. In the event of a cyberattack, financial support from cyber insurance can help ensure business continuity.

Compliance and legal requirements. Some industries and jurisdictions may require that businesses have cyber insurance as part of regulatory compliance.

Costs of data breaches. The price associated with these incidents can be substantial, including legal fees, fines, and loss of business. Cyber insurance helps mitigate these costs.

Reputation management. Cyber insurance often includes services for managing the fallout of a cyber incident, which can be crucial in preserving a company's reputation.

Increasing threat landscape. As the digital landscape

evolves, the risk of cyber incidents also increases, making insurance more relevant.

In some cases, obtaining cyber insurance can be challenging. Firms will send a detailed questionnaire asking for detailed descriptions of your current cyber-security program and controls in place. They may visit the business to validate the responses provided in the questionnaire. Here are some of the challenges that businesses have faced in obtaining cyber insurance:

Underwriting process. This can be complex. Insurers assess the cyber-risk profile of a business, including evaluating existing cybersecurity measures and past incident history.

Rising premiums and stringent requirements. Due to the increasing number of cyber incidents, insurers are raising premiums and may impose stringent cyberse-curity requirements.

Varied coverage. Policies can vary significantly be-tween providers, so finding the right coverage can be challenging.

Evolving cyber threats. The constantly changing na-ture of cyber threats can make it difficult for insurers to assess risk and for businesses to maintain coverage that remains relevant.

Limited understanding. Some businesses might find it difficult to understand the nuances of the cyber insurance market, making it challenging to select appropriate coverage.

Industry-specific risks. Certain industries may face more challenges in obtaining cyber insurance due to the higher risk factors associated with their operations.

While cyber insurance is not universally necessary for every business, it is increasingly becoming an important consideration—especially for those handling sensitive data or operating in high-risk industries. The difficulty in obtaining it varies based on the business's risk profile and the evolving nature of cyber threats. Businesses should assess their specific risk exposure and consult with insurance experts to determine the best course of action.

Disaster Recovery Plan

There are many different names for disaster recovery scenarios, including continuity of operations (COOP) and business resiliency. All are meant to keep businesses running during a major event or following some catastrophe. Many businesses already have disaster recovery plans in place for things like hurricanes, earthquakes, fires, and other types of natural disasters. Creating a disaster recovery plan specifically for a cyberattack, and more specifically for ransomware, should be added to that list.

Creating a ransomware disaster recovery plan requires a multifaceted approach. To ensure an organization can effectively respond to and recover from a ransomware attack, it's crucial to understand some key considerations:

Risk assessment and analysis. Assess the organization's vulnerability to ransomware attacks. Identify critical assets and systems that could be targeted.

Preventive measures. Implement strong cybersecurity practices like regular software updates, firewalls, and antivirus software. Conduct employee training on recognizing and avoiding phishing emails and other common attack vectors.

Data backup strategy. Regularly create copies of critical material and ensure these are stored in a separate and secure location. Test backups frequently to ensure data integrity and recovery capabilities.

Incident response plan. Develop a comprehensive reaction blueprint that includes procedures for isolating affected systems, notifying stakeholders, and contacting law enforcement if necessary. The FBI's cybercrime unit is great and can be reached via the web at <www.ic3.gov>. Also, assign roles and responsibilities for team members during a ransomware incident.

Recovery procedures. Establish a clear process for restoring systems and information from backups. Plan for different scenarios, from partial to complete data loss.

Communication plan. Prepare talking point templates for internal and external stakeholders, including employees, customers, and media. Ensure clarity regarding who will communicate what and when during a crisis.

Legal and compliance considerations. Understand the legal implications of a ransomware attack, especially regarding notification laws. Consult with legal experts to navigate the complexities of paying or not paying a ransom.

Cyber insurance. As described above, evaluate the need for cyber insurance to cover potential financial losses due to a ransomware attack.

Testing and drills. Regularly conduct simulations and drills to test the effectiveness of the disaster recovery plan and do so at least annually. Update the plan based on lessons learned from these exercises.

Post-incident analysis. After an incident, thoroughly

analyze what happened and why. Make a recovery plan to address any identified weaknesses.

Collaboration with external experts. Consider partnerships with cybersecurity firms or experts who can provide additional support and expertise. One consideration is to give a retainer to a cybersecurity incident response firm. By doing this in advance, all the paperwork and contracts are already reviewed by legal teams and in place. Then, if an event occurs, the cybersecurity firm can respond quickly, typically within 24 hours.

By integrating these considerations into a ransomware disaster recovery plan, organizational resilience is strengthened and more effective responses are ensured.

What to Do When a Ransomware Attack Occurs

CONTAIN THE INCIDENT

Immediately isolate the affected systems to prevent the further spread of ransomware. This includes disconnecting the infected devices from the network and Wi-Fi, as well as any external storage devices. It is often a good practice during a cyberattack to disconnect networks from the internet. The public-facing website can just post a notice saying you are down for scheduled maintenance and will be back soon, or something similar that is approved by the legal and communications team. By cutting off access to the internet, a hacker who is actively diving into the network is cut off, too.

SECURE THE BACKUPS

Check backups to ensure they are unaffected and secure. Do not connect backup drives or access backup systems until you are sure they are not compromised.

ASSESS THE SITUATION

Determine the scope of the attack, including which systems are affected and the type of ransomware involved. It's crucial to identify whether it's a known ransomware variant as this might influence the response strategy.

NOTIFY RELEVANT PARTIES

Inform the internal IT team and management (and the MSSP if there is one). Depending on the severity and immediate legal requirements, you may also need to notify law enforcement, customers, and regulatory bodies.

CONSULT CYBERSECURITY EXPERTS

Engage with IT security professionals or a cybersecurity firm specializing in ransomware (as described above). They can provide guidance on whether to pay the ransom, how to remove the ransomware, and how to restore systems.

THE RANSOM

This is a business leadership decision. Paying the ransom does not guarantee the return of data and may encourage future attacks. However, in some cases, businesses may consider paying the ransom—particularly if the cost will be covered by cyber insurance.

RESTORE FROM BACKUPS

If backups are secure and up to date, begin the process of restoring data and systems from these backups.

STRENGTHEN SECURITY MESASURES

After resolving the immediate crisis, review and update cybersecurity measures. This includes employee training, updating software, improving backup procedures, and implementing robust security protocols.

LEARN FROM THE INCIDENT

Conduct a post-incident review to understand how the attack happened and how similar incidents can be prevented in the future.

COMPLIANCE AND LEGAL CONSIDERATIONS

Ensure compliance with any legal or regulatory requirements related to data breaches, which may include specific reporting timelines and notifications.

Conclusion

In summary, ransomware—a type of malware that encrypts files and makes them inaccessible—requires a ransom to be paid that may or may not result in the delivery of a decryption key. Impacts range from the loss of critical data and financial losses to disruption of operations and damage to an organization's reputation.

Businesses need to have a preparedness plan for cyber incidents, as well as regularly training staff in cybersecurity best practices. By taking these measures, businesses can significantly reduce their risk of suffering a ransomware attack and minimize any impact if one does occur. Protecting against ransomware is crucial because attacks can have devastating consequences for individuals and organizations.

Combatting ransomware requires essential steps, such as regularly updating and patching systems, implementing strong cybersecurity measures like firewalls and antivirus software, and educating employees about how to prevent phishing scams. In the event of an attack, immediate steps include disconnecting infected systems from the network, assessing the extent of the damage, and contacting law enforcement. It's also vital to have a robust backup strategy that includes secure, up-to-date backups that may be an effective way to restore data without paying a ransom. Additionally, developing and practicing a comprehensive incident response plan can significantly mitigate the damage caused by ransomware attacks.

CHAPTER 17

Business Email Compromise

A sophisticated scam targeting businesses that regularly perform wire transfer payments, business email compromise (BEC) is carried out by compromising legitimate business email accounts through social engineering or computer intrusion techniques to conduct unauthorized transmittals. Quite often it occurs via a successful phishing attack.

For example, an employee in an organization receives an email. They click on a link and, poof, malware is downloaded to the system. Typically, the malware will "phone home" via the internet to the hacker, who then gets to work searching for key individuals in the business. Hackers love to find the CEO and CFO email accounts because then they can send emails within the organization—or even to external vendors or partners. Good hackers hide their tracks very well. No one can find the email in a Sent Items folder or Deleted Items folder. They also create rules inside the mailboxes so that, if anyone responds to their bogus email, the rule will auto-forward it to the hacker and delete the original reply so the real CEO or CFO isn't tipped off.

Once in an email account, where do hackers go? What's most important to them? Probably not the in-box—it probably has a lot of spam and other useless email. Contacts? Again, probably not. Because this data might not be helpful to a hacker right away. The answer is the Sent Items folder.

This is ground zero for the hacking victim. They have been responding to employees, vendors, part-ners, lawyers, etc. Hackers can often find things like invoices, bank account information, wire transfer doc-uments, and sensitive subjects the company wouldn't want to be made public. Another reason is they can mimic the language this senior person uses, which will make the sham emails that hackers will send from this email address more believable. Maybe the person has a unique greeting, ending, or way of writing; hackers can then copy and paste language from a stolen email to mimic the senior person's communication style. There are several types of BEC scams. All of them are usually discovered only after the money has been transferred and has "flown the coop":

CEO FRAUD

Impersonating a high-level executive (like a CEO), then instructing employees—often with a sense of urgency—to transfer funds or send sensitive data. The insistence and confidentiality of the request puts pressure on the recipient to act quickly.

The language used is authoritative and plays on the employee's sense of loyalty. As stated above, the cybercriminal might also copy the executive's own words from another email. The email address might be spoofed to look incredibly similar to the real one, or the attacker may have gained control of the actual account via hacking.

The unsuspecting employee, believing they are following a direct order from the CEO/CFO, initiates the transfer to the bank account specified by the scammer.

FAKE INVOICE SCHEME

In this case, a scammer poses as a supplier and requests fund transfers for invoices to a fraudulent account. The scam begins with cybercriminals either hacking into or spoofing the email account of a company executive or vendor. They typically use phishing techniques to gain access to legitimate email credentials.

Once they have access, they monitor correspondence to understand the payment processes, billing cycles, and key personnel involved in financial transactions. They then create a convincing fake invoice from the legitimate vendor using logos, language, and even bank account details that have been slightly altered.

The fraudulent invoice is sent to the person responsible for wire transfers within the target company. The email usually includes a message indicating that the vendor has changed its bank account details and that future payments should be sent to this account. Often, the email will stress the urgency of making payment and may ask to keep any account changes confidential. This is to prevent the target from verifying the new account details through other communication channels.

ACCOUNT COMPROMISE

Here, an employee's email account is hacked and used to request invoice payments to vendors listed in the email contacts that the cybercriminals have gained access to.

The first step is often through phishing, with an employee tricked into revealing their login credentials or malware infiltrating the system. Once hackers have control of the email account, they impersonate the account's owner. This can be a high-level executive, any employee, or a trusted vendor.

The attacker sends emails to other employees, customers, or vendors associated with the company that typically request wire transfers or payments to a new account. Since the emails come from a legitimate account, they seem credible. The unsuspecting recipient, believing the request to be legitimate, transfers funds to an account controlled by the criminal.

ATTORNEY IMPERSONATION

Scammers have also been known to impersonate a lawyer or legal representative, one who is supposedly in charge of crucial and confidential matters—usually at the end of the business day—to pressure employees into transferring funds for some urgent matter.

The scammer, posing as the attorney, contacts either the CEO or a responsible employee (usually in finance) via email. They create a sense of urgency and stress the need for secrecy, claiming the matter is sensitive or under a strict deadline. This pressure tactic is intended to prompt a hasty decision without proper verification.

Their email will instruct the victim to wire funds to an account for a seemingly legitimate purpose, such as settling a confidential legal matter, a transaction requiring immediate action, or a sensitive financial operation. This account is usually offshore and controlled by the scammer.

Due to the supposed sensitivity of the request, the email may discourage the recipient from using other communication channels to confirm the request. This lack of verification plays into the scammer's hands.

DATA THEFT

Attackers gain unauthorized access to a company's email accounts to steal sensitive material. By targeting human resources or finance departments, personally identifiable information (PII) or tax statements can be found that are then often used in future attacks.

Attackers begin by compromising email accounts within an organization. Once access has been attained, hackers spend time monitoring communications to understand the company's operations, hierarchy, and ongoing transactions. This surveillance helps them identify what is most valuable and what is the best time to strike.

The attackers then steal sensitive material like financial information, employee personal records, proprietary business intelligence, customer data, and more. They might download documents, forward emails to themselves, or use the compromised account to request material from other employees.

Skilled attackers might try to cover their tracks by deleting sent emails or altering log files, making it harder for the company to detect and understand the full scope of the breach.

In some instances, the attackers might use the stolen material to extort money from the company, threatening to release the information publicly or sell it to competitors unless a ransom is paid. In other cases, data gleaned from one company's emails can be used to launch targeted attacks against its partners or customers.

Data theft can have significant consequences for businesses, including financial loss, reputational damage, and legal implications.

Real Estate is an Especially Common Target

Business email compromise is a significant concern during real estate transactions. This is due to the large monetary values typically involved in real estate transactions and the reliance on email communication, not to mention there is often time-related pressure on transactions. BEC scammers exploit the various communications between parties—title companies, agents, and escrow companies—and impersonate individuals or entities involved in the title and closing processes, manipulating victims to transfer funds to fraudulent accounts.

One real-world example occurred in Edwardsville, Illinois. A real estate agent named Shawn sent closing instructions to the buyers. Subsequently, the buyers received an email, seemingly from Shawn, instructing them to wire the closing amount of $303,855.50 immediately to avoid delays. This email, however, was not from Shawn. A scammer was using a fake email address and account. Fortunately, the buyers brought a cashier's check to the closing instead of wiring the money, averting a potential financial loss.[24]

Another case, reported by CNBC, involved a son who won a house auction in Texas for his elderly parents. Before the closing, he received an email, ostensibly from his real estate agent, with changes regarding the instructions for wiring funds. Trusting the authenticity of the email, the son transferred funds to the new bank details provided. It was only on the closing day, when the title company followed up for payment, that the scam was uncovered.[25]

These examples highlight the vulnerability of real estate transactions to BEC scams. They emphasize the importance of verifying any changes in payment instructions directly with the concerned parties to prevent such fraud.

Protection Against Email Being Compromised

To defend against BEC, businesses can take several steps:

Educate employees. Regular training about recognizing phishing emails and verifying email requests for

---

[24] "Business Email Compromise Scam Full Study," Better Business Bureau, n.d., accessed January 9, 2024. https://www.bbb.org/all/scamstudies/bec_scams/bec_scams_full_study.

[25] "'Business Email Compromise'" Attacks: What They Are and How You Can Avoid Them," CRES, n.d., accessed January 9, 2024. https://www.cresinsurance.com/business-email-compromise-attacks-how-you-can-avoid/.

transfers of funds or confidential information is crucial.

Dual-approval verification. Implement a dual-approval verification process for financial transactions, such as phone confirmation using known numbers—and not numbers provided in an email request. Even if the email appears to come from the CEO or CFO, there should be a second review of the transaction before it gets approved and money is sent.

Two-factor authentication (2FA). Use 2FA for accessing business email accounts to add an extra layer of security.

Email security measures. Implement email security systems that can detect weaponized emails, domain spoofing, and other red flags.

Review financial practices. Establish internal procedures that require multiple approvals for wire transfers and regularly review them.

Conclusion

By staying vigilant and implementing strong security practices, businesses can significantly reduce their risk of falling victim to business email compromise scams. Protecting against them is crucial due to the significant financial and reputational impacts on organizations that can result, with losses that can run into millions of dollars.

BEC scams involve the impersonation of company executives or business partners to trick employees into transferring money or sensitive information. Additionally, BEC attacks expose vulnerabilities in an organization's security protocols and internal controls, highlighting the need for robust cybersecurity measures and employee awareness training. By safeguarding against BEC, businesses can prevent financial loss, defend sensitive data, and maintain their reputation and customer confidence.

CHAPTER 18

Working from Home in the Cloud

COVID-19 pushed more businesses to adopt remote work options. The pandemic acted as a catalyst in accelerating trends in this direction that were already underway due to technological advancements. This shift is likely to have long-lasting effects on how businesses operate.

The pandemic coincided with significant advancements in technology, making remote work more feasible. Tools for communication, collaboration, and cloud services saw rapid improvement and adoption.

Many employees found remote work to be more flexible and convenient, leading to a shift in work culture. Businesses had to adapt to these preferences to attract and retain talent. For companies, remote work expanded the trend to tap into a global workforce not limited by geographic boundaries. Companies also realized cost savings in terms of reduced office space, utilities, and other overhead. Some businesses saw increased productivity from employees when working remotely, further encouraging this shift. Remote work also reduces environmental impacts by cutting down on commuting and, in the event of emergencies or unexpected situations, it ensures that business operations can continue uninterrupted.

Remote access solutions, which come with robust security features to ensure data remains secure even when accessed from outside the office, can be easily scaled up or down, making them suitable for businesses of all sizes and adaptable to changing business needs.

The benefits are obvious. However, there are significant security concerns requiring adherence to security precautions that mitigate risks. One of the first considerations is whether a business is going to issue company-owned laptops to employees or create a bring your own device (BYOD) environment that allows employees to work remotely using their personal devices. Technology solutions for each scenario are different.

Company-Owned Devices

Security on company-owned devices is generally much higher. They are typically equipped with preinstalled security measures maintained by the company's IT department. They follow standardized security protocols and software configurations set by the company. The organization can monitor these devices and regularly update security software, thereby retaining more control over what is stored on and accessed from these devices.

A company-owned device should use virtual private network (VPN) software for remote access. A VPN creates a secure tunnel between the user's device and the company's network that encrypts data and hides IP addresses.

Personally Owned Devices

Employee-owned, personal devices may have varying levels of security, depending on the user's habits and installed software. Some employees allow their children to use their personal computer for games or internet browsing, which is not a great scenario. The company has limited control over these devices, making it harder to enforce security protocols. These kinds of risks mean there's a higher chance that sensitive company intelligence is compromised or mixed with personal data.

Companies allowing personal devices often implement BYOD policies to set guidelines for usage and security. One of the most important is not using VPN remote access. Instead, use either a virtual desktop infrastructure (VDI) or remote desktop services (RDS). VDI and RDS offer several advantages for remote access in a BYOD environment:

Centralization. Centralize both processing and storage at the data center rather than the individual's device. This minimizes the risk of a breach if a BYOD device is lost or stolen. The data and applications remain on the servers, providing a layer of security against unauthorized access.

Flexibility. Both are largely device agnostic, allowing users to access their desktops and applications from any device, be it a laptop, tablet, or smartphone. This is particularly beneficial in a BYOD setting, where there's a wide variety of devices and operating systems.

Simplification. These systems streamline the management of applications and desktops. IT administrators can manage, update, and troubleshoot systems centrally without needing to physically access each BYOD device. Such central management reduces the complexity and cost of maintaining a diverse array of user devices.

Consistency. Both provide a consistent user experience regardless of the access device being used. Users get the same interface, applications, and performance, enhancing productivity and reducing learning curves for new software or updates.

Computing power. Since processing is done on

centralized servers, the individual user's device doesn't need to be as powerful. This makes it easier to accommodate a wide range of devices under a BYOD policy since performance is more dependent on the network and servers than on the local device.

Cost-effectiveness. In the long term, the practice of centralizing applications and desktops reduces the need for high-end hardware on the user's end and can lower software licensing costs.

Scaling. Both environments can be scaled up or down based on the organization's needs. This is crucial in adapting to changing workloads and the varying number of users in a BYOD environment.

Protection. For industries that require adherence to strict data protection and privacy regulations, VDI and RDS offer better compliance capabilities. Since data is stored centrally and not on individual devices, it's easier to implement and monitor compliance policies.

VDI and RDS provide robust, secure, and flexible solutions for remote access in a BYOD environment, offering advantages in security, management, user experience, and cost-effectiveness.

Additional Security Precautions for Remote Access

Secure internet connection. Use a secure, private Wi-Fi network. Public networks should be avoided due to security vulnerabilities.

Strong passwords and two-factor authentication (2FA). Strong, unique passwords coupled with 2FA add layers of security, making unauthorized access more difficult.

Regular software updates. Ensure that all software, including antivirus and anti-malware programs, are up to date to defend against the latest threats.

Firewalls and antivirus software. Use firewalls to protect network boundaries and antivirus software to scan for malware.

Secure file sharing and storage. Use encrypted file-sharing services and secure cloud storage to safeguard sensitive data.

Employee training. Educate employees about cyber-security best practices, including recognizing phishing attempts and safe internet habits.

Limit access. Implement least-privilege access controls, ensuring employees have access only to the information necessary for their job roles.

Cloud-Based Services

A viable and often beneficial option for small to midsize businesses is cloud-based services that offer several advantages, while also presenting some challenges. Advantages include:

Cost-effectiveness. Cloud services often have scalable pricing models that make them affordable for SMBs. You pay for what is used, avoiding the high upfront costs of on-premise solutions.

Scalability and flexibility. They allow businesses to easily scale up or down based on their needs. This is especially useful for SMBs that experience fluctuating or growing demands. Cloud services enable remote access to data and applications, facilitating collaboration among employees who might be spread across different locations.

Access and collaboration. Cloud providers typically handle maintenance and updates, reducing the burden on internal IT staff.

Maintenance and updates. Many cloud services include robust backup and disaster recovery solutions, which can be costly to implement on-premise.

However, there are some considerations to think about:

Security. While cloud providers often have strong security measures, their shared nature can present risks. It's crucial to understand the security protocols of the provider and ensure they align with business needs. Major cloud service providers are very secure. However, applications, systems, and datasets can be misconfigured. It's imperative to have an IT team or an MSP experienced in cloud security to ensure data and systems are properly managed.

Compliance. Depending on the industry, there may be regulations regarding the storage and handling of data, like GDPR and HIPAA. Ensure the cloud service complies with relevant regulations.

Dependency on internet connectivity. Cloud services require a reliable internet connection and interruptions can impact access to critical business functions.

Data control. There's a degree of control surrendered when using cloud services. It's important to understand how data is managed and what happens in the case of a dispute or service termination.
Long-term costs. While initially more cost-effective,

long-term use of cloud services can sometimes become expensive. It's important to monitor and manage usage to avoid cost overruns.

Finally, all access to cloud services must have two-factor authentication enabled. All connections to and from the cloud service location must have HTTPS enabled so that data traversing from the user to the cloud (and vice versa) is fully encrypted. Ideally, users should always have a VPN enabled when accessing the cloud.

For SMBs, cloud-based services offer flexibility, scalability, and potential cost savings. However, it's crucial to choose a reputable provider, understand the terms of service, and consider any industry-specific compliance requirements. Regularly reviewing and assessing the cloud strategy in relation to business needs and growth are also essential.

Conclusion

While remote access is feasible and often necessary, it requires a robust security framework, especially in the context of diverse device ownership. Ensuring the security of both company and personal devices through a combination of technology and employee training is critical for safe and effective remote work.

For company-owned devices, using a virtual private network (VPN) is essential. VPNs create a secure, encrypted connection over a less secure network (in this case, the internet). This ensures that sensitive company data remains protected from unauthorized access.

On the other hand, in bring your own device (BYOD) scenarios, solutions like virtual desktop infrastructure (VDI) or remote desktop services (RDS) are more suitable. These technologies provide a virtualized environment separating the company's material from the personal data on the employee's device. This setup not only enhances security by isolating the business environment from the personal, it also offers flexibility and convenience to employees who prefer working on their own devices. Both strategies—VPNs for company devices and VDI/RDS for BYOD—address the unique challenges of remote access, ensuring that businesses maintain robust security standards while accommodating different working arrangements.

CHAPTER 19

Many Businesses Need Social Media

I t is okay for a business to use social media; in many cases, it's highly beneficial. Social media platforms can be powerful tools for marketing, brand building, customer engagement, and market research.

But if something goes wrong, it can go wrong fast. If, while you're asleep, hackers on the other side of the world get control of a social media account you may wake up to find the company's reputation has been set on fire by someone taking this powerful public-facing communication tool for a joyride. Or sensitive information has been compromised and getting things back under control will come with added expenses.

Build a thorough defense

There are certain precautions businesses should take to ensure their social media usage is secure and effective:

DEVELOP A SOCIAL MEDIA POLICY

Having a business social media policy is crucial in today's digital landscape. It serves as a framework for how employees conduct themselves online, particularly when representing the company, and as a training aid. This helps protect the company's reputation by preventing inappropriate or damaging posts. It also ensures that the communication aligns with the company's values and marketing strategies. Additionally, a well-defined social media policy can provide legal defense by clearly outlining what is acceptable, thereby reducing legal risks stemming from social media use. Finally, it encourages responsible use of social media, which can enhance the company's brand and foster positive engagement with customers.

In essence, a social media policy is not just about limiting risks; it's also about leveraging social media effectively to support the company's goals and image.

TRAIN STAFF

Training employees on best practices for using social media, including understanding privacy settings, recognizing phishing attempts, and the importance of not sharing sensitive company data, is crucial:

Reputation Safety. It helps in safeguarding the company's reputation. Employees, being representatives of the organization, can inadvertently cause reputational harm through inappropriate or misinformed posts.

Guardrails. Training equips employees with the knowledge of what constitutes acceptable and professional behavior online and how to align their social media activities with the company's values and policies. This is particularly important as the boundaries between personal and professional online presence often blur.

Stay on the Right Side of the Law. Employee education reduces the risk of legal issues related to privacy, confidentiality, and compliance with various laws and regulations.

Positive Results. Trained employees can use social media effectively as a tool to enhance the company's brand, engage with customers, and potentially drive business results.

Make Things Better. Good social media behavior promotes a safer and more respectful online environment for everyone, both within and outside an organization.

SECURE ACCOUNTS WITH STRONG PASSWORDS

Use strong, unique passwords for each social media account and change them regularly. Consider using a password manager and enable two-factor authentication where available.

MONITOR ACCOUNTS REGULARLY

Regular monitoring of business social media accounts is crucial:

Work in real time. Businesses can engage promptly and effectively with their audience, build stronger relationships, and enhance customer satisfaction. Immediate responses to queries or complaints can significantly improve the customer experience.

Support the brand. Regular monitoring helps in maintaining a positive brand image. By keeping track of mentions and feedback, businesses can address negative comments or misinformation quickly, preventing potential damage to their reputation.

Insight. Valuable insights regarding customer preferences and market trends can inform marketing strategies and product development.

Stay relevant. A consistent social media presence via regular monitoring ensures a business remains relevant and at the forefront of its audience's attention.

Catch attacks early. Regular monitoring can help to quickly identify and respond to unauthorized access or inappropriate content posted on accounts.

Stay informed. Identifying and leveraging opportunities for growth, such as potential collaborations or emerging market segments, contribute to the overall success and sustainability of a business.

LIMIT ACCESS TO SOCIAL MEDIA ACCOUNTS

Limiting social media privileges to a few trusted employees is crucial.

Consistency. Ensures coherent messaging and brand representation. Fewer people posting means messages are more likely to stay on-brand and aligned with company values. This consistency is key to building a reliable and professional brand image.

Reduce risk. Less chance of security breaches and the spread of misinformation. With fewer individuals having access, the chances of unauthorized posts or security compromises decrease significantly.

Simplicity. Monitoring and accountability are more straightforward. When only a handful of trusted employees manage social media, it's easier to track who posts what and to hold individuals accountable. This streamlined approach leads to more efficient and effective social media management, safeguarding the company's public image and reducing potential legal and reputational risks.

REGULARLY UPDATE SECURITY SETTINGS

Social media platforms often update their security features. Make sure to regularly review and update security settings to protect accounts.

HAVE A CRISIS MANAGEMENT PLAN

Having a plan in place for how to respond on social media to a security breach or public relations crisis is crucial. This should include steps for communication both internally and externally. This is important for several key reasons:

Fast and broad communication. Social media's expansive reach and ability to rapidly spread information can amplify a crisis. Using it to make a swift and effective response is essential to mitigating damage.

Real-time communication. Platforms can be used for real-time communication with stakeholders, enabling businesses to provide updates, clarify misinformation, and maintain trust. A well-crafted plan ensures a coordinated and consistent message, which is vital in maintaining the organization's reputation and public image.

Better understanding of public sentiment. A good social media crisis management strategy helps in understanding public sentiment, allowing businesses to adapt their responses appropriately.

Stay cool. It helps an organization handle a crisis more efficiently, reducing internal panic and confusion while promoting a more professional and controlled external response.

In the digital age, with social media significantly influencing public perceptions, being unprepared can lead to long-lasting negative impacts on a business's reputation and financial health.

OTHER BEST PRACTICES

Stay informed about the latest security threats. Social media platforms are constantly evolving—and so are security threats that target them.

Use verified accounts. If possible, get the business's social media accounts verified. This adds a level of authenticity and trust for your audience.

Regularly back up content. In case of account compromise or data loss, having backups of social media content can be invaluable.

Contact info. Do not post the actual email address or phone numbers of employees. Use generic ones like <info@mybusiness.com> or <contact@mybusiness.com>. Use the central phone number for the business rather than individual lines. Posting personal email addresses and phone numbers makes those individuals targets for phishing, smishing, and vishing schemes.

By implementing such precautions, a business can effectively utilize social media while minimizing the risks associated with it.

Conclusion

Securing a business's social media presence is crucial for several reasons: First, it protects the company's reputation since these platforms are key points of contact with customers and the public. Any compromise can lead to the spread of falsehoods or negative perceptions. Second, it safeguards sensitive information. Businesses often share and store some confidential material through social media, and breaches can lead to theft or loss. Third, a secure social media presence helps to prevent financial losses. Cyberattacks can result in direct financial damages and costly recovery processes and compliance with data protection regulations, which can vary greatly depending on the region and industry, is important.

Finally, by demonstrating a business's commitment to defending their interests, robust security fosters trust among customers and stakeholders.

In the digital age—where social media is a vital part of business strategy—securing that online presence is not just a technical issue but a cornerstone of business integrity and continuity.

CHAPTER 20

Critical: Secure Your Wi-Fi Networks

C hapter 7 discussed Wi-Fi considerations for the home. This chapter explores things specific to Wi-Fi networks, which have become a basic part of the business infrastructure. Office Wi-Fi networks, like any other, can be hacked, potentially leading to serious security breaches.

Precautions Businesses Can Take

Not securing a company's network is business malpractice. Protecting a business's internal network and internet connection is a 24/7 responsibility and taking shortcuts is inviting disaster. Here are the steps to take:

WI-FI NAMING CONVENTIONS

Most offices will have two or more Wi-Fi networks, the main network that allows access to business systems and data and usually a guest or visitor network. A good practice is not using the name of a business on any Wi-Fi network. Use nondescript names.

Guest network. On the guest network, do not use the word guest. If a hacker sees <guest>, they won't be interested and will look even harder to find the main network.

Main network. Using a business name as part of a Wi-Fi title is saying to cybercriminals, "Here is my company, please come and attack it." When a hacker sees a business name, they can google it and discover a lot of information before determining if it is a worthwhile target. Don't give them that opportunity.

I was once meeting with a client about cybersecurity. We were in the boardroom with many senior executives and the IT team; we were all sitting on the second floor of the building overlooking the parking lot. On the wall in the back of the room was a sign reading <businessname_guest> and the password.

I was talking about Wi-Fi configuration settings and the importance of naming conventions. I pointed at the sign, then looked out the window and saw a van in the parking lot. Pointing to the van, I said there could be hackers sitting in that van right now. "If they can see your Wi-Fi networks, they can hack them," I told the group. The general counsel started shaking his head and I asked him what was wrong. He replied that the company's main Wi-Fi network was named the same way, <businessname_main>. We renamed their networks that day.

In a multistory building, there could be hackers on the floor above or below your office, or maybe out in the lobby near the elevator. Again, if they can see the network on their screens, they can hack it.

Another question I am often asked is whether to hide the Wi-Fi network name—the service set identifier (SSID)—and thus make it unreadable. This is certainly an option, but hackers have tools that scan nearby airwaves for wireless networks. They will see the names of other wireless networks and any networks without names. That's going to pique their curiosity and make them wonder why that business is hiding their network. What is so valuable that they don't want to broadcast the name? I think it's just better to broadcast a nondescript name and not draw attention to yourself.

ACCESS CONTROL

Implement access-control measures for all Wi-Fi networks, using the following tactics.

1. ONLY COMPANY-OWNED DEVICES

On the main network, only company-owned devices should be able to connect to it. If an employee wants to check their email or social media on a personal device, they can do so on the guest network. You don't know if personal devices have a virus or malware on them; however, the IT team ensures that company-owned devices have antivirus/anti-malware software.

2. MAC ADDRESS FILTERING

Every network-enabled device has a unique hardware identifier called the media access control (MAC) address and filtering involves creating a list of those allowed on the router or access point. MAC address filtering is simple to implement but can be cumbersome to maintain, especially in networks with many devices, and is therefore more common in smaller networks.

When a device attempts to connect to the network, the access point checks its MAC address against the list. If it is on the list, access is granted; if not, access is denied. This method is less secure than certificate-based authentication since MAC addresses can be spoofed (faked) relatively easily, which can allow unauthorized devices to gain access. Often used in small networks or home environments. It's a basic form of access control that can be combined with other methods, like WPA3 encryption, for increased security.

3. CERTIFICATE-BASED AUTHENTICATION

This method uses digital certificates for authentication, a digital form of identification that acts like a passport or driver's license. It includes the user's or device's public key and is issued by a trusted authority known as a certificate authority (CA).

When a device tries to connect to a Wi-Fi network, it presents its certificate. If the certificate is valid and trusted, access is granted. This method is considered highly secure because it's difficult to forge a certificate, thus reducing the risk of unauthorized access. Commonly used in enterprise environments where high security is a priority, it's suitable for scenarios with many users.

Certificate-based authentication is more secure than MAC address filtering. It's harder to bypass and provides stronger assurance of the identity of connecting devices, is more complex to set up and manage, and requires a system to issue and revoke certificates. Certificate-based authentication is more suited for larger, more security-conscious environments like businesses or educational institutions.

STRONG ENCRYPTION

Use WPA3 encryption, which is considered the best encryption standard for Wi-Fi networks due to several key improvements over its predecessor WPA2. It offers enhanced defense against offline dictionary attacks using "simultaneous authentication of equals" (SAE), a more secure handshake protocol[26]. This makes it much harder for attackers to crack passwords by repeatedly trying different combinations.

WPA3 provides increased privacy on open networks through individualized data encryption, ensuring that Wi-Fi network transmissions are uniquely encrypted for each user—even on networks that don't require a password. This feature, known as opportunistic wireless encryption (OWE), significantly enhances user privacy. Another feature, forward secrecy, prevents attackers, who have captured encrypted data from a Wi-Fi network, from decrypting past sessions—even if they eventually crack the network's password. Finally, WPA3 includes a 192-bit security suite aligned with the Commercial National Security Algorithm Suite (CNSA) that provides a

---

[26] Handshake protocol is a protocol for establishing a secure connection between a client and a server. It is intended to verify the authenticity and security of the channel being set up and includes a series of control procedures to keep intruders out.

higher level of security for government, defense, and industrial networks.

These features collectively make WPA3 the most robust and secure Wi-Fi encryption standard available, offering superior protection against a range of cyber threats.

DISABLE WPS

Wi-Fi Protected Setup (WPS) should be disabled for several security reasons. Initially designed to simplify the process of connecting devices to Wi-Fi networks, it allows users to connect by pushing a button or entering an eight-digit PIN. However, this convenience comes at a price.

The WPS PIN is a significant vulnerability, susceptible to brute-force attacks. Since the PIN is only eight digits—and the last digit is a checksum (a sum to assure that data is free from errors or tempering)—the number of attempts needed to guess it is significantly reduced. Moreover, some routers expose the first and second halves of the PIN separately, further simplifying a brute-force attack. Once the WPS PIN is compromised, an attacker can gain access to the Wi-Fi network, potentially intercepting sensitive data or launching further attacks.

SECURE PASSWORDS

Implement strong, complex passwords and change them regularly. Avoid using default passwords that come with the hardware, as hackers can easily find default passwords on the internet.

Strong passwords on Wi-Fi routers are essential for several reasons. First, they secure the network against unauthorized access, preventing outsiders from using the internet connection without permission. This is important not only to defend bandwidth and prevent unauthorized network congestion but also to avoid any illegal activities being conducted on your network. Second, strong passwords safeguard personal and sensitive information.

Without a robust password, hackers can intercept financial data, personal emails, or passwords. Additionally, a secure Wi-Fi network is crucial for protecting against various cyber threats like malware and ransomware. In summary, a strong password is a fundamental layer of defense that ensures the security and privacy of your digital life.

NETWORK SEGMENTATION

Separate the network into different segments. For instance, have different Wi-Fi networks for guests, employees, and management—each with different access levels and permissions. Network segmentation is crucial for enhancing security and improving network performance. It isolates sensitive data and systems from general network traffic, reducing the risk of cyberattacks and breaches. This segmentation allows for better control over who has access to specific parts of the network, thereby safeguarding critical information.

Additionally, it manages network traffic more efficiently, preventing any single device from overloading the network. This is particularly important in environments with a high number of connected devices or where sensitive data is regularly transmitted. Furthermore, in the event of a security breach, network segmentation limits the extent of the breach, as attackers cannot access the entire system. This compartmentalization also simplifies troubleshooting and maintenance, as issues can be localized and addressed more efficiently.

REGULAR UPDATES

Keep the router's firmware and any associated software up to date to ensure that security patches are applied. Best practice is to replace the Wi-Fi routers about every three years. Not only are there new security technologies but operating speeds also increase. Replacing the devices gives you better security and better performance.

VPN USAGE

Encourage or mandate the use of virtual private networks (VPNs) for remote access to the office network. This adds an extra layer of encryption and security.

WI-FI FIREWALL AND INTRUSION DETECTION SYSTEMS

These monitor and defend the network from unauthorized access.

1. WI-FI FIREWALL

Serves as a barrier between a secure internal network and a non-trusted external network, like the internet. It monitors and controls incoming and outgoing traffic based on predetermined security rules. These firewalls can be hardware-based, software-based, or a combination of these and often include features like packet filtering, IP address blocking, and domain name system (DNS) filtering.

2. INTRUSION DETECTION SYSTEMS (IDS)

Designed to detect and alert administrators about potential security breaches, such as malicious activities or policy violations. There are two main types of IDS: Network-based intrusion detection systems (NIDS) monitor network traffic for suspicious activity, while host-based intrusion detection systems (HIDS) monitor a single host for signs of malicious activity. These systems use various methods to detect intrusions, including signature-based detection, which compares network activities against a database of known threat signatures, and anomaly-based detection, which identifies deviations from a baseline of normal activity.

Both Wi-Fi firewalls and IDS play a crucial role in maintaining the security integrity of wireless networks, safeguarding sensitive data, and preventing unauthorized access.

IT providers can set these up for SMBs. If maintaining a small network, the default configuration of the Wi-Fi firewall should be sufficient. If not an enterprise Wi-Fi router, it may not have a wireless intrusion detection system.

EDUCATE EMPLOYEES

Regularly educate employees about the importance of network security, safe browsing practices, and the risks of connecting unknown devices to the network.

PERFORM REGULAR SECURITY AUDITS

Conduct regular security audits and penetration testing to identify and fix vulnerabilities.

USE SECURE PROTOCOLS

The use of secure protocols in online communications is crucial for ensuring data integrity, confidentiality, and authentication. Protocols like HTTPS and SFTP, which are secure versions of HTTP and FTP respectively, encrypt data during transmission, preventing unauthorized interception and access.

This is particularly important for sensitive

information, such as personal details, financial information, and login credentials. On the other hand, unsecured protocols like HTTP and FTP do not provide encryption, making data transmitted over them vulnerable to eavesdropping, man-in-the-middle attacks, and tampering. The lack of security in these protocols can lead to significant risks. Consequently, shifting to secure protocols is essential to safeguarding users and maintaining the integrity of online interactions in our increasingly digital world.

PHYSICAL SECURITY

The physical security of Wi-Fi routers and network devices in a business setting is crucial. These devices are the gateways to an organization's network. If compromised, unauthorized individuals can gain access to sensitive data, disrupt business operations, and launch cyberattacks. Physically securing these devices helps prevent tampering, theft, or unauthorized access. It also protects against risks like accidental damage or environmental hazards.

By ensuring that devices are securely housed, and that access is controlled, businesses can mitigate risks associated with breaches and network downtime. Effective physical security forms a vital part of a comprehensive cybersecurity strategy, complementing digital safeguards and ensuring the integrity and reliability of infrastructure.

Conclusion

With these measures, a business can significantly enhance the security of its office Wi-Fi networks and defend against potential cyber threats. Properly securing Wi-Fi routers in a business setting is crucial for several reasons.

First, it helps shield sensitive business material from unauthorized access and cyberattacks like hacking or data theft. An unsecured network is an open invitation for cybercriminals to intercept confidential intelligence. Additionally, a secure Wi-Fi network ensures the integrity and availability of the business's internet connection, which is essential for the smooth operation of daily activities. It also prevents the network from being used for illegal activities that could potentially implicate the business in criminal activities. Securing the Wi-Fi router also helps in maintaining compliance with data protection regulations regarding the handling of customer or client information.

Overall, the security of Wi-Fi routers is a fundamental aspect of a business's overall cybersecurity strategy, safeguarding both the business and its stakeholders from a myriad of digital threats.

CHAPTER 21

Third-Party Risk

S mall-to-midsize companies must take into consideration how best to keep their business safe and well-protected from cybersecurity threats, including those originating from third-party vendors that have access to another company's sensitive data. To mitigate this, businesses should ensure that vendors implement robust cybersecurity measures, conduct regular security audits, and insist on compliance with industry-standard security protocols. If they don't, then don't grant them access to your networks—and maybe find a company that better understands doing business in the 21st century.

There are operational risks associated with a vendor's ability to deliver services or products, including cybersecurity. This could be due to financial instability, supply chain issues, or lack of competency. Businesses should evaluate the operational stability and track record of vendors and have contingency plans in place.

Reputational risk is a concern as well. The actions or misconduct of a third party can flow downhill onto other businesses, damaging their reputation. Close monitoring of vendors' practices and ensuring they align with the company's ethical standards can help mitigate this risk.

External Best Practices

CONDUCT THOROUGH VETTING

SMBs can effectively reduce third-party risk by implementing a comprehensive vetting process, including conducting thorough background checks on potential third-party partners and assessing their financial stability, reputation, and compliance with relevant laws and industry standards. Businesses should also evaluate the third party's data security measures and cybersecurity certifications, such as SSAE18 SOC II, Type II, or ISO27001, as well as their history of handling sensitive information. Cybersecurity is a critical aspect of third-party risk.

IMPLEMENT STRONG CONTRACTS

It is crucial to meticulously craft and implement robust contracts with detailed service-level agreements (SLAs) and compliance requirements. Ensure that they include clear terms regarding performance expectations, compliance requirements, data security, and other relevant standards. This should include several key steps.

Clearly defining the scope of work, responsibilities, and expectations in a contract ensures both parties have a mutual understanding of their roles. Given today's digital landscape, detailed security and privacy clauses should be included to safeguard sensitive information and mitigate cybersecurity risks.

It's also important to include well-defined termination clauses and dispute resolution mechanisms to handle potential issues efficiently. Keeping these contracts up to date with evolving industry standards, legal requirements, and business needs will maintain strong and effective third-party risk management.

REGULAR MONITORING AND AUDITING

Continuously monitor and audit the performance and compliance of third-party vendors. This can involve regular reviews, audits, and feedback sessions involving consistent evaluation and oversight of external partners, suppliers, and service providers. By establishing a rigorous monitoring system, businesses can identify potential risks and vulnerabilities in their supply chain or service delivery.

Regular audits, both internal and by third parties, play a crucial role in ensuring that external entities comply with contractual obligations, industry standards, and regulatory requirements. These audits should assess the security, quality, and reliability.

Additionally, they help maintain clear communication channels and build performance metrics that can help to quickly address any issues that arise. By adopting a proactive approach to monitoring and auditing, businesses can mitigate risks, maintain operational integrity, and safeguard their reputation.

Internal Best Practices

DEVELOP A RISK MANAGEMENT PLAN

Outline the procedures for managing third-party risks. Effective communication channels should be established for reporting and resolving issues. Additionally, businesses should have contingency and mitigation plans in place for various scenarios like data breaches or service disruptions. This plan should be regularly reviewed and updated to adapt to new risks and changes in the business environment.

Contingency plans should identify and evaluate key vendors and service providers that are integral to the company's operations and any potential risks associated with each of them, including the possibility of vendor failures or disruptions.

Such planning could include establishing alternative sources or backup vendors and outlining specific response procedures in the event of a disruption. Businesses must ensure continuity and resilience to minimize the impact of third-party vulnerabilities. Such a strategic approach can safeguard against unforeseen cyber challenges and contribute to building a more reliable and sustainable business model.

EDUCATE EMPLOYEES

Train employees on the risks associated with third-party interactions and how crucial the importance of adhering to internal policies and procedures is to success. This involves developing comprehensive training programs. Employees should be made aware of how third-party actions can impact the business, including potential legal, financial, and reputational risks.

Key elements should include identifying red flags, understanding compliance requirements, and learning about the data security and privacy concerns associated with third parties. Regular updates and refreshers are crucial to keep knowledge current. Additionally, creating a culture of responsibility in which employees feel empowered to report suspicious activities or concerns can significantly mitigate risks. This approach not only educates employees but fosters a proactive stance toward managing third-party relationships effectively.

LEVERAGE TECHNOLOGY

Utilize tech solutions for better risk assessment and monitoring, including software for contract management, compliance tracking, and risk analysis. Using advanced software tools, businesses can automate and streamline the process of identifying potential risks associated with their vendors and partners.

This includes algorithms to analyze the financial stability, compliance record, and cybersecurity posture of third parties. Continuous monitoring tools can also alert businesses to any changes in the risk profiles of their partners, enabling timely responses to emerging threats. Such solutions can facilitate better data management and integration, ensuring that risk-related information is centralized, up-to-date, and easily accessible for decision-making. These technologies not only mitigate risks but can also improve overall operational efficiency and compliance with regulatory standards.

REVIEW AND ADAPT

Regularly review and update third-party risk management policies and practices to adapt to new threats, regulatory changes, and evolving business needs. This proactive approach is important for keeping up with an ever-changing landscape that is characterized by new threats, regulatory changes, and evolving business needs. By staying updated, businesses can ensure that their policies remain relevant and effective in identifying, assessing, and mitigating risks associated with third-party vendors and partners.

Rules of Third-Party Access

If granting a third-party access to a network, make sure the process is strictly controlled:

In-house devices. Consider issuing them a company laptop for access since you can control the security measures on that device. However, many times this is not feasible.

Control the avenue of access. Use virtual desktop infrastructure (VDI) or remote desktop services (RDS)—or even a secure portal—to provide access, but only to specific files, folders, or locations that require access.

Two-factor authentication. As always, all access must use two-factor authentication and must be closely monitored. In some cases, access operations can be recorded.

If sharing data with a third-party provider, make sure they perform cybersecurity due diligence:

Know their track record. Use a reputable firm that has been in business for some time and, as mentioned above, ask about their cybersecurity policies and procedures.

Proper procedures. Do they have an international

security certification, such as SSAE18, SOC 2 Type 2, or ISO 27001, or any other internationally recognized cybersecurity certification? This will show if they understand due diligence when handling data.

Know their procedures. What are their notification procedures if they suffer a cybersecurity breach?

Encryption. Most businesses don't encrypt all their information in the cloud because it can get very expensive, so many identify the most sensitive or critical cloud data and then encrypt only that. But everything that is being sent up to the cloud or downloaded from it must be encrypted using HTTPS while in transit.

Conclusion

These steps can significantly reduce SMBs exposure to third-party risks and safeguard their operations and reputation. They must prioritize protection against third-party risks for several crucial reasons since they often have limited resources and may lack the robust security infrastructure of larger corporations. These limitations make them more vulnerable to risks posed by third parties like suppliers, vendors, or partners.

Third-party risks can manifest themselves in various forms, including cybersecurity threats, compliance issues, operational disruptions, and reputational damage. When SMBs engage with third parties, they may inadvertently expose themselves to these risks. Defending against them helps SMBs shield data, maintain compliance with regulations, ensure operational continuity, and preserve their reputation in the marketplace. Additionally, as SMBs come to increasingly rely on digital networks and transactions, the potential impact of third-party risks grows, making proactive risk management an essential component of overall business strategy.

Chapter 22

Ensuring Secure Communications

Whenever transmitting sensitive information it's crucial to use secure communications that protect data from being intercepted by cybercriminals and defend it from unauthorized access, theft, or interception. This is essential to maintaining confidentiality and integrity of data.

Many industries are governed by strict regulations regarding privacy and security, such as GDPR in the European Union, HIPAA in the US health-care sector, and various other national cybersecurity laws. Secure communication is often a legal requirement of such regulation.

It also helps maintain trust with clients, partners, and employees and demonstrates a commitment to upholding privacy standards. Ensuring the security of communications helps maintain the smooth operation of business processes and safeguards against disruptions caused by cyberattacks.

Yes, Email is Convenient But...

Email is the least desirable method to transmit sensitive documents. If you must use it, make sure to use an encryption application for not only the body of the email but all attachments as well. If sending a password-protected document via email, do not send the password in a subsequent email. If a hacker can intercept the first email with the attachment, they'll also be grabbing that second one, too. Use another type of communication—a secure text message or, ideally, just a phone call—to let the recipient know the document has been sent and then give them the password.

Here are several secure communication methods, including the sharing of documents:

ENCRYPTION

Encryption is crucial. It ensures privacy and data security by converting information into a coded format that is unreadable to unauthorized users. Encryption acts as a vital defense against breaches, eavesdropping, and cyberattacks, plus it secures sensitive material like financial details, personal material, and confidential communication by requiring a decryption key to unscramble the original document.

This is especially important in scenarios like online banking, confidential business communications, and preventing identity theft and fraud. Encryption also plays a key role in maintaining the integrity of data, which ensures that it has not been altered or tampered with during transmission.

Overall, encryption is an essential component of trust and security in the digital age, allowing individuals and organizations to communicate and transact safely over potentially insecure networks like the internet. Encrypting data during transmission (SSL/HTTPS for web traffic; other encryption applications for emails) ensures that, even if intercepted, the information remains unreadable to unauthorized parties.

VIRTUAL PRIVATE NETWORKS (VPN)

VPNs create a secure and encrypted tunnel for transmission, providing protection from eavesdropping or interception, especially on public networks. Using a VPN is crucial for secure communications for several reasons:

Encryption. Data being transmitted over the internet is encrypted. This is particularly important when using public Wi-Fi networks, which are often less secure and more susceptible to breaches.

Hiding IP addresses. A VPN masks the user's IP address and location, enhancing privacy and anonymity online. This is beneficial for shielding personal identity and browsing history from being tracked by websites, internet service providers, and potentially intrusive government surveillance.

More freedom. VPNs enable access to geo-restricted content, empowering users to bypass internet censorship and access a broader range of information and services.

Overall, VPNs are a key tool to enhance digital security, preserve privacy, and ensure freedom of access in the increasingly interconnected and digitally monitored world.

SECURE PORTAL

Using a secure portal is considered the best method for safeguarding communications. They typically offer a user-friendly interface, which makes them easier for nontechnical users. They can be integrated with other business systems for streamlined workflows and can send notifications when documents are uploaded or downloaded. Other key factors include:

Encryption. Secure portals employ robust encryption, making it nearly impossible for unauthorized parties to decipher. This is particularly important for sensitive information exchange.

Authentication. With strong authentication mechanisms, users are required to verify their identity through methods like two-factor authentication, which adds an extra layer of security.

Strict access. These portals typically have strict access controls, allowing only authorized users to view or manipulate data, thereby reducing the risk of breaches.

Compliance. Secure portals are designed to comply with various data protection regulations, which ensures legal adherence and enhances trust among users.

Logs. Audit trails and activity monitoring enable administrators to track access and any changes to data, which is crucial for identifying and mitigating potential security threats.

Overall, secure portals provide a comprehensive and robust framework for ensuring the confidentiality, integrity, and availability of communications.

Secure File Transfer Protocols

This is an older technique requiring that users have more technical knowledge. It's helpful when users need to send very large files or a very large volume of files. Using secure protocols like secure file transfer protocol (SFTP) or secure copy protocol (SCP) for file transfers adds a layer of security compared to standard file transfer protocol (FTP), which should not be used because it is an unsecured protocol. In fact, many businesses block the FTP protocol on their networks.

End-to-End Encryption (E2EE)

Services that offer end-to-end encryption, such as certain messaging apps, ensure that only the sender and the recipient can access the contents of a message. While E2EE apps provide a strong level of security, they are not foolproof. Overall security depends on various technical and human factors. Regular updates, strong user practices, and understanding the limitations of the technology are key to maintaining security.

Two-Factor Authentication

Implementing two-factor authentication for accessing communication tools adds an additional layer of security beyond just passwords.

Email Security Measures

Secure email gateways are a foundational measure, acting as intermediaries to filter out spam, phishing attempts, and malware from incoming and outgoing emails. These gateways scrutinize email content for suspicious elements, offering a robust first line of defense. Encrypted email services take security a step further by encoding the contents of emails, making them unreadable to anyone except the intended recipient. This encryption can be end-to-end, ensuring that emails are secure from the moment they are sent until they are decrypted by the recipient. Additionally, digital signatures authenticate the sender's identity, confirming that the email has not been altered in transit, which helps maintain the integrity of the message and builds trust in digital communications.

Working together, these measures form a comprehensive approach to safeguarding email communication against various cyber threats, ensuring the confidentiality, authenticity, and integrity of the messages.

Secure Collaboration Tools

Designed to facilitate teamwork while ensuring the confidentiality and integrity of the material shared among team members, these tools are crucial for several reasons:

Encryption. End-to-end encryption ensures that only intended recipients can access transmitted information, thus securing sensitive data from unauthorized access, including from service providers.

Features. They often include options like secure file sharing, video conferencing, secure file storage, and real-time messaging (essential in today's digital workplace, especially with the rise of remote work).

Compliance. Help with various data regulations, like GDPR, by providing secure and compliant ways to store and share information.

Protection. Secure collaboration tools can prevent breaches and cyberattacks.

Company culture. A culture of security within organizations is fostered by making employees more aware and vigilant about defending sensitive material.

Regular Audits and Updates

Communication tools that feature regular auditing and updating play a crucial role in ensuring secure communications. They help identify and rectify vulnerabilities that could be exploited by hackers or malware and, as technology evolves, counter emerging security threats. This is especially important in sectors handling sensitive data, where lapses in security can have serious consequences.

Updates often include patches for newly discovered vulnerabilities and are critical for maintaining the integrity and confidentiality of communications. Regular updates also ensure compatibility with the latest technologies and standards, which can enhance the efficiency and reliability of communication systems.

Finally, audits and updates demonstrate a commitment to security that can boost client and stakeholder trust.

Each of these methods addresses different aspects of communication security and are often used in combination to provide comprehensive protection for sensitive business data.

Conclusion

Secure communications are vital for businesses to guard sensitive material, maintain confidentiality, and ensure data integrity. This defense is essential to prevent unauthorized access, breaches, and cyberattacks that could lead to financial loss, legal consequences, and damage to the company's reputation. They also comply with various privacy laws and regulations, ensuring that customer and client materials are handled responsibly.

Robust communication security fosters trust among stakeholders, including employees, customers, and partners, by demonstrating a commitment to safe-guarding their data. In an era when information is a critical asset, the importance of secure communications to a business cannot be overstated.

CHAPTER 23

Antivirus/Anti-Malware Software

Businesses of all sizes need to have robust antivirus/anti-malware software on all their devices, including servers, workstations, laptops, tablets, and cellphones. Antivirus/anti-malware software helps defend this sensitive data from theft, corruption, or loss due to malicious software (malware) that can lead to significant system downtime. In an interconnected environment, malware on one device can quickly spread to others. Comprehensive security is necessary to safeguard the entire network. Effective antivirus solutions can prevent disruptions by detecting and removing threats before they cause harm.

Many industries have regulations requiring businesses to protect customer data. Failure to comply can result in significant repercussions. SMBs are increasingly targeted by cybercriminals because they often have weaker security compared to larger enterprises. Antivirus/anti-malware software helps level the playing field.

Put Security Measures in Place

Consider implementing an enterprise-grade antivirus/anti-malware solution across the entire business organization. This is one area where a business should not cut corners to save money. At the time of this writing, Microsoft offers different levels of its Windows Defender for Endpoint protection: E3 and E5.

While both E3 and E5 offer robust endpoint protection through Microsoft Defender, the E5 plan provides more advanced features, such as automated response, threat hunting, and comprehensive identity protection, which provides the much more sophisticated security solution needed in today's ever-changing cyber threat environment.

For effective defense, an antivirus/anti-malware solution should include the following features:

REAL-TIME SCANNING

This is a critical component of antivirus and anti-malware solutions because it offers immediate defense against threats by continuously monitoring for suspicious activities, files, or processes. This is essential in a landscape where malware and viruses are becoming increasingly sophisticated and can quickly cause significant damage. Real-time scanning helps prevent the execution of malicious activities before they can spread or infect other files. It offers peace of mind since systems are being actively safeguarded at all times, even as new threats emerge.

MULTILAYERED MALWARE DETECTION

Utilizing a combination of detection methods (heuristics, behavior analysis, and signature-based detection) to identify and neutralize threats. Each layer targets specific types of malware or attack vectors, thereby increasing the overall detection rate and reducing the chances of malware slipping through undetected.

For instance, signature-based detection excels at identifying known malware, while heuristic analysis can detect novel threats by analyzing behaviors and anomalies. Machine learning algorithms can adapt and improve over time, identifying patterns that human analysts might miss. This layered strategy provides redundancy, so if one layer fails or is bypassed, others can still wall off the system.

A multilayered approach ensures a more dynamic and proactive defense, making it harder for attackers to exploit a single point of failure.

AUTOMATIC UPDATES

Regularly updating virus definitions and software capabilities is crucial for maintaining effective defense against evolving cyber threats. As hackers and cyber-criminals continuously develop new methods to evade detection, outdated antivirus software may not recognize newer threats—leaving systems vulnerable to attacks.

By updating regularly, antivirus software keeps an up-to-date database that includes the latest virus signatures and malware behaviors, which enhances the identification and neutralization of threats. Software updates also often include patches for recently discovered vulnerabilities in the antivirus program itself.

This ongoing process of updating ensures that antivirus software remains effective.

EMAIL DEFENSES

Scanning emails and attachments for malware, especially a "sandbox" feature that analyzes links, is a critical component of an antivirus or anti-malware solution. Email is a common vector for cyberattacks, where malicious actors use phishing, spear-phishing, and using other deceptive tactics to trick users into downloading malware or revealing sensitive information. By scanning emails and attachments, such a system can identify and neutralize threats before they compromise the user's device or network.

The sandbox feature analyzing links adds an extra layer of security. When a user clicks a link, it is isolated and analyzed in a controlled setting. The safety of the website it leads to is assessed, protecting users from accessing potentially harmful sites.

Scanning collectively enhances the overall security posture, safeguarding both individual users and organizational networks from a wide range of email-based threats.

WEB DEFENSES

Blocking access to malicious websites is a crucial component of any antivirus or anti-malware solution. This feature serves as a first line of defense against a variety of online threats.

By preventing users from accessing dangerous websites, it significantly reduces the risk of, for instance, a drive-by download,[27] where a website can secretly install harmful software on a user's device without their knowledge. This is particularly insidious because it can bypass user interaction—the user doesn't have to do a thing—making proactive blocking essential.

Web protection helps safeguard sensitive personal and financial information. Overall, incorporating it into antivirus solutions not only enhances the security

---

[27] A drive-by download is where a user goes to a website and does not know that a page on the website has been compromised by a hacker who has embedded malware into a picture file on the page. Picture files on websites automatically download to temporary folders on a system. If malware is in one of these picture files, when it downloads it will run and try and take over the system.

posture of an individual or organization but also contributes to a safer overall online experience.

FIREWALL INTEGRATION

This enhances security by creating an additional layer of defense against external threats. Firewalls monitor and control incoming and outgoing network traffic based on predetermined security rules, effectively preventing unauthorized access and potential attacks.

The integration of a firewall with antivirus software ensures a more comprehensive security perimeter. While antivirus programs are adept at detecting and removing malicious software on a device, firewalls provide proactive protection by blocking malicious traffic and unauthorized connections before they reach any device. The synergy between the two types of software significantly reduces a system's vulnerability to a wide range of cyber threats, which simplifies security management for users and administrators. It provides a unified security solution that is easier to manage and monitor, ensuring that all aspects of network and system security are covered under a single, cohesive strategy.

CENTRALIZED MANAGEMENT

By simplifying monitoring, IT administrators can oversee the security status of all devices within the network from a single dashboard. This unified view enables quicker detection and response to security threats and ensures that all devices are adhering to consistent security policies.

This enhances efficiency, as administrators can deploy updates, patches, and new policies across the entire network simultaneously, rather than the time-consuming task of managing each device individually. This also reduces the risk of human error. Centralized management also facilitates comprehensive reporting and analytics, providing valuable insights into network health and potential vulnerabilities.

DATA LOSS PREVENTION (DLP)

These tools are crucial for antivirus and anti-malware solutions because they play a key role in shielding sensitive information from unauthorized access, loss, or theft. Designed to detect and prevent potential leakage of critical data—whether from external threats like malware and hacking or through internal sources like employee negligence or misconduct—it is part of an integrated, comprehensive security posture.

DLP tools ensure that sensitive data remains within the secure perimeter of the organization, reinforcing overall security. This is increasingly important since regulatory compliance demands stringent protection measures.

COMPATABILITY AND PERFORMANCE

Compatible   antivirus   programs   integrate

seamlessly with operating systems and other software, minimizing the likelihood of errors or crashes. This is particularly important when many users are running a variety of applications simultaneously and disruptions will lead to losses of productivity and/or data.

Maintaining high performance while running efficiently is vital because antivirus programs need to continuously scan and monitor system activities without consuming excessive system resources. Resource-intensive antivirus solutions can significantly slow down a computer, affecting the user's experience and potentially leading to frustration or even disabling the antivirus program in frustration. Efficient performance ensures that the system remains responsive and that the antivirus functions are carried out in the background, which provides protection without a noticeable impact on the system's performance. This balance of security and usability is key to the effectiveness and user acceptance of an antivirus solution.

SUPPORT AND TRAINING

Support and training are crucial components of an antivirus/anti-malware solution; they play a pivotal role in enhancing cybersecurity.

Reliable customer support ensures that users receive timely assistance for any issues or queries they encounter, contributing to a more secure and efficient use of software. This aspect is particularly important in rapidly addressing and mitigating the impact of cyber threats.

Equally important, the provision of resources for educating employees about cybersecurity best practices empowers them to recognize potential threats, understand the importance of regular updates, and adhere to safe online practices.

This dual approach of robust support and comprehensive training not only maximizes the effectiveness of the antivirus solution but also fosters a more security-conscious culture within organizations, reducing the likelihood of breaches and enhancing overall cyber resilience.

Conclusion

Collectively, well-designed antivirus/anti-malware software systems ensure a robust security posture for businesses, defending them from a wide array of cyber threats while maintaining operational efficiency. Such software plays a crucial role in safeguarding against various cyber threats that can compromise sensitive data, disrupt operations, and inflict financial and reputational damage. Businesses of all sizes need to have this software on all their devices, including servers, workstations, laptops, tablets, and cellphones.

These tools provide a defense against malware—including viruses, worms, spyware, and ransomware—that can infiltrate systems and then encrypt data, steal information, spy on business activities, or damage IT infrastructure. They also help comply with legal and regulatory requirements.

In an era when cyber threats are increasingly sophisticated and frequent, antivirus and anti-malware solutions are essential for maintaining business continuity, securing customer trust, and protecting intellectual and financial assets.

CHAPTER 24

Two-Factor Authentication (2FA)

There's a reason why two-factor authentication (2FA)—also known as multifactor authentication (MFA) and two-step verification—has been mentioned throughout this book. It is absolutely one of the best and most important ways to ward off attacks.

By requiring two different authentication factors, 2FA adds an additional layer of security to the basic single-factor authentication (basically just a password). It is designed to increase the security of a user's credentials and the resources they can access.

2FA Everywhere, All the Time

Two-factor authentication must be enabled on everything, including log-ons for your:

- Remote access

- Email accounts
- Business networks
- Cloud environments
- Bank accounts
- Anywhere else it is offered

Some business organizations have 2FA enabled internally on their networks as well. For example, an employee logs into the network (via 2FA) and works normally. Then they decide to go to an intranet portal within the organization. To do so, they must be authenticated again with 2FA. This may seem like an inconvenience to users, but this technique defends against an insider threat if a hacker has compromised a user's account. They can't get to any of the other portals because they would not have the second factor of authentication.

Here's why 2FA is crucial, particularly in a business context:

ENHANCED SECURITY

The use of two-factor authentication significantly restricts the likelihood of unauthorized access to business accounts. The core principle is the requirement of two distinct forms of verification before access is granted.

Typically, this involves something the user knows, like a password, and something the user possesses, like a mobile device that receives a unique code, or something the user is, like biometrics. The key advantage is that, even if a password is compromised, the likelihood of an attacker also having access to the second factor is low. This added layer of security makes it vastly more challenging for attackers to breach accounts.

NO PHISHING ACCESS

Using 2FA adds an additional layer of defense against unauthorized access. Even if an attacker manages to obtain a user's password, they still face the significant hurdle of needing to bypass the second factor to gain access. This dual-layer protection makes it considerably more difficult for attackers to compromise accounts.

COMPLIANCE REQUIREMENTS

Compliance requirements like HIPAA (Health Insurance Portability and Accountability Act), PCI-DSS (Payment Card Industry Data Security Standard), and GDPR (General Data Protection Regulation) mandate or strongly recommend two-factor authentication as a critical security measure.

The primary reason is to enhance the security of sensitive data, which is a central concern for these regulations. 2FA is well-known for significantly reducing the risk of unauthorized access. For businesses, adhering to these standards is crucial to meeting regulatory compliance requirements.

REDUCED FRAUD AND IDENTITY THEFT

With 2FA in place, users must provide two different forms of identification before gaining access to their account. This makes it much harder for attackers to impersonate a user. By ensuring that only the rightful user can access an account, 2FA plays a crucial role in safeguarding against unauthorized access and identity theft.

BUILDING TRUST

Two-factor authentication significantly enhances trust between businesses and their clients or partners by showcasing a strong commitment to security. A business not only adds an extra layer of defense to sensitive data and transactions but also visibly prioritizes the safety of its stakeholders' information.

In a world where cyber threats are increasingly sophisticated, the adoption of 2FA by a business sends a clear message to its clients and partners that it is serious about defending their property.

Versatile Options for Authentication

There are several enhanced security measures via 2FA to protect sensitive data and user accounts. The most common is SMS-based 2FA, where a code is sent to the user's mobile device. Although widely used due to its simplicity and ease of implementation, this is the least secure option. It is highly recommended to use another method, thanks to hackers' ability to intercept

SMS codes (as discussed in Chapter 9). Better methods include:

Third-party apps. Authentication apps like Microsoft Authenticator, Google Authenticator, or Authy generate time-based one-time passwords (TOTPs) without the need for a network connection.

Hardware tokens. YubiKeys, for example, provides a physical device that generates a login code, offering another layer of security.

Biometric 2FA. Fingerprints, facial recognition, or other biometric data are increasingly popular for their unique user identification capabilities.

Email-based 2FA. Businesses can utilize a system where codes are sent to the user's email address.

Each of these methods provides a different balance of convenience, cost, and security, allowing businesses to choose the most suitable option for their specific needs and risk profile.

Adapting to Evolving Threats

As cyber threats evolve, relying solely on passwords is increasingly insufficient. 2FA provides a more robust defense against a variety of attack vectors. It has evolved significantly to the rapidly changing landscape of cyber threats.

Initially, security relied mainly on passwords, but as these became increasingly susceptible to attacks like phishing and brute-force attempts, the need for an added layer of defense became evident.

However, as threats continue to evolve, so too must 2FA technologies. This need for evolution is evident in the emergence of adaptive authentication strategies that combine various factors and intelligence types to provide dynamic and robust protection. These strategies also pave the way for a future where "passwordless" authentication might become the norm via increasingly familiar methods like biometrics, thus making the authentication process more seamless and secure.

Overall, the adaptation of 2FA and its evolution into more sophisticated MFA forms is a critical response to the escalating complexity and frequency of cyber threats. As digital connections increase and threats become more advanced, the role of these authentication methods will continue to grow, underscoring their importance in modern cybersecurity.

Conclusion

Two-factor authentication is one of the most critical security measures for businesses in today's digital landscape, as it significantly enhances the security of user accounts beyond the traditional single password by requiring two different forms of verification: something the user knows (like a password) and something the user has (such as a mobile device for a text message or a security token) or something the user is (biometrics like fingerprints or facial or iris recognition).

This dual-layer approach adds an extra barrier against unauthorized access, making it considerably more challenging for attackers to breach accounts, even if they have obtained the password. At a time when cyber threats are increasingly sophisticated, 2FA helps safeguard sensitive business data, maintain customer trust, and comply with regulatory requirements.

CHAPTER 25

Control Internet Access

After email and phishing, internet browsing is the next dangerous environment for businesses to navigate. Access to webpages needs to be monitored and controlled to make sure that employees do not go to inappropriate sites or inadvertently download malware from a malicious or compromised website.

Filtering employees' internet access aims to enhance productivity, security, and compliance with regulations. Limiting access to sites not related to work, such as social media or entertainment platforms, can reduce distractions and ensure that employees focus on their tasks.

It reduces the risk of malware and phishing attacks as well. In addition, certain industries are required to comply with regulations regarding internet usage to prevent access to inappropriate content or secure sensitive information.

Don't Open the Data Faucet

Ways to regulate internet access include:

Limiting access to high-bandwidth sites. Blocking sites such as video streaming services ensures that the company's internet resources are used efficiently and don't slow down network speed.

Restricting certain websites. Preventing access to controversial or inappropriate websites can safeguard a company's public image. Access to illegal or inappropriate content can lead to legal issues.

Restricting access across the board. Unrestricted internet access increases the amount of cybersecurity threats and the likelihood of security breaches. Also, doing so can increase productivity.

Web content filtering can include various methods, such as URL filtering, IP filtering, keyword filtering, and file-type filtering. Each serves a specific purpose, like blocking inappropriate or malicious websites, restricting access to certain IP addresses, searching for specific words or phrases to block certain types of content, and controlling the types of files that can be accessed or downloaded.

Here are some of the most common solutions in

use today to take control of internet access via a network:

SOFTWARE SOLUTIONS

By installing web filtering software on company networks, specific categories of websites or specific URLs can be blocked. Several firms offer businesses cloud-based web filtering services with updated databases of categorized websites and flexible policies.

In coordination with human resources and legal teams, a business can determine what types of sites to block. Typical categories include adult (pornography), drugs, gambling, hacking, terrorism and hate, gaming, peer-to-peer (P2P), and 80-plus others.

One category that must be blocked is unknown or uncategorized. There are billions of websites on the internet with more being created every day, including a host of malicious websites developed by hackers. Because these websites are brand new, they have not yet been categorized. That's why it's so important to block access to them. An employee can easily click on a phishing email link that goes to one of these new, uncategorized websites. Occasionally, there are false positives. In those one-off cases, the IT team can add access to that site once it is verified.

HARDWARE-BASED SOLUTIONS

These typically involve using specialized devices like firewalls, routers with advanced filtering capabilities, or dedicated web filtering appliances. This is often a more robust solution than using software, but it can be more expensive. Such tools are designed to monitor and control internet traffic flowing in and out of a business's network.

Key features include the ability to block access to specific websites or categories of content, enforce internet usage policies, protect against web-based threats, and manage bandwidth usage. Some advanced devices also offer detailed reporting and analytics that can help administrators understand web usage patterns and optimize network performance.

Such hardware solutions are less prone to being bypassed and can handle a higher volume of traffic. However, they may require more upfront investment and technical expertise to deploy and manage effectively.

CUSTOMIZABLE POLICIES

This involves setting up different levels of access for various employee groups, an approach recognizing that different roles within an organization may require varying degrees of internet access.

For instance, a marketing team might need broader access to social media platforms than the finance department. Customizable policies allow for flexibility. This can include restricting access to potentially harmful or non-work-related websites, thereby enhancing productivity and mitigating security risks.

Additionally, these policies can be adjusted to

adapt to changing business needs or evolving online threats. Implementing such policies often requires a combination of hardware and software solutions, along with clear guidelines and regular monitoring to ensure compliance and effectiveness.

REGULAR AUDITING AND UPDATING

Doing this ensures the continued effectiveness of systems in blocking inappropriate or harmful content, thereby maintaining a safe and professional work environment.

Regular updates are essential to keep up with the constantly evolving landscape of internet threats. This helps safeguard the company's data and employees' personal information from cyber threats.

Auditing allows businesses to review and adjust access controls as necessary, ensuring that they are neither too restrictive, which could hinder productivity, nor too lenient, which could expose the company to risks.

Compliance with legal and industry standards is often a requirement, and regular auditing helps in adhering to these regulations. Overall, this practice plays a vital role in maintaining a balance in workplace security, compliance, and productivity.

EMPLOYEE TRAINING AND AWARENESS

Such efforts educate employees about the risks associated with unfiltered internet access, including exposure to malicious content, phishing scams, and potential data breaches. Understanding the reasons behind internet filtering policies helps employees recognize the importance of adhering to the guidelines, thereby fostering a culture of security and responsibility. Training also empowers employees to identify and report suspicious activities, contributing to the overall safety of the IT environment.

In essence, effective employee training and awareness initiatives are fundamental to reinforcing a company's cybersecurity framework and ensuring a safe, secure, and productive work environment. Informed employees are more likely to respect and comply with policies because they understand both what's expected and why.

Conclusion

Implementing internet filtering requires a balance between security, productivity, and employee morale. Overly restrictive policies can frustrate employees; too-lenient policies might not effectively mitigate risks. It's important for businesses to tailor their approach based on their specific needs and industry requirements.

Blocking access to potentially harmful websites reduces the risk of threats like malware or phishing attacks. It can also boost productivity and help enforce company policies regarding acceptable use of the internet. By controlling bandwidth usage, filtering ensures that critical business operations get the necessary bandwidth. It's a key component in managing the digital workplace, safeguarding company assets, and promoting a productive and secure working environment.

CHAPTER 26

No, They Don't Need User Admin Rights

Normal business routines for most employees do not require system or network administrative privileges or capabilities. Admin rights should be strictly limited and doing so is a crucial aspect of cybersecurity and overall IT management.

Limiting admin rights maintains control over the IT environment and reduces the risk of security breaches. Users with admin rights can install software, change system settings, and access sensitive data. If such a user's account is compromised, then hackers have far more power on their hands.

In addition, regular users—especially those who are not tech-savvy—might unintentionally change important settings or install harmful software. I have seen instances of an employee going to a website and downloading what they think is a productivity app that has malware or adware embedded in it. Limiting admin rights mitigates the risk of this kind of mistake. If an employee needs to download an application, have a protocol in place that requires they first submit a request to the IT team, who will test it to make sure it is safe to install.

Keep It Simple

Fewer users with admin rights means the IT department can more easily manage and monitor systems and ensure that updates and security policies are consistently applied. Here are some tips about limiting admin rights:

ROLE-BASED ACCESS CONTROL

Role-based access control (RBAC) is a widely used method for regulating access to computer systems and data, based on the roles of individual users. Users are granted permissions based on their roles within an organization.

All employees in departments like HR, legal, and sales have a designated level of rights and access, which is more efficient and secure than assigning permissions to individual users.

For instance, an employee in the HR department might have access to the personal data of employees, but not to financial records. This ensures that users have access only to the information and resources necessary for their job functions, which reduces the risk of accidental or malicious breaches.

RBAC is flexible and can be easily adjusted as roles change within an organization. It simplifies the management of user permissions, leading to a more secure and efficient administration of system privileges.

USE OF ADMINISTRATIVE ACCOUNTS

In a business setting, controlling the use of administrative accounts is crucial to maintaining security and operational integrity. It is recommended that businesses create separate user accounts for individuals who require occasional administrative access that is distinct from their regular user accounts. This approach ensures that administrative privileges are granted only when necessary and are not used for everyday tasks.

This reduces the risk of accidental or malicious changes to critical system settings. It also aids in tracking and auditing administrative actions, as the use of these accounts can be closely monitored. Implementing such a policy not only enhances security but also fosters a more disciplined and responsible use of administrative privileges within the organization.

AUTOMATED SOLUTIONS

Due to their complexity and scale, identity and access management (IAM) solutions are vital for larger organizations. These automate the managing of user identities and access rights, streamlining what would otherwise be a cumbersome and error-prone manual process. Using predefined policies, IAM systems ensure that access rights are granted or revoked in accordance with organizational requirements and compliance standards.

This not only enhances security by reducing the risk of unauthorized access but also improves efficiency since it allows for quick and accurate updates to user privileges in response to role changes or other organizational shifts. IAM solutions also provide comprehensive auditing and reporting capabilities, which are essential for regulatory compliance and security monitoring. Several firms offer cloud-based services that easily scale.

REGULAR AUDITS AND REVIEWS

Inspecting administrative accounts is essential for maintaining security and operational efficiency. Audits should be routine to ensure timely detection of any anomalies or unauthorized access. The process typically involves verifying the legitimacy and necessity of all administrative accounts and ensuring that each account is used only for its intended purpose.

It's important to review and update access permissions regularly to align with changes in job roles and responsibilities. This includes checking for accounts associated with former employees or accounts that have unusual levels of access. The audit process should be well-documented, including the date of the review, findings, and any actions taken. This ensures account-ability and provides a historical record for future audits.

Additionally, employing tools for automated monitoring and alerts can complement these reviews by providing ongoing oversight and early detection of potential security breaches.

EMPLOYEE TRAINING

Educating employees about the risks associated with administrative rights is crucial for maintaining the security and integrity of an organization's IT infrastructure. This is part of fostering a culture of security awareness and making employees realize that admin rights must be used responsibly and only when necessary. This training also helps in complying with various regulatory standards that mandate strict control over access to sensitive information, protecting not only the organization's assets but also the interests of its customers and stakeholders.

WINDOWS SYSTEM SETTINGS

These are two settings in Windows that can be used to limit admin rights.

Group Policy

A powerful tool for centralized management and configuration within an Active Directory environment. Group policy allows administrators to control and standardize various aspects of operating systems, applications, and user settings across multiple computers and users. This is achieved through a set of rules or policies, which are applied to groups of users or computer accounts within a domain.

Group Policy can enforce security settings, software installations, and user interface settings, ensuring that all machines and users adhere to the organizational standards and security protocols. It can also be used to restrict administrative privileges, which limits users' ability to make changes that could affect network security or stability. This feature is especially important in large organizations where maintaining a consistent and secure computing environment is crucial.

With Group Policy administrators can efficiently manage many computers and users, reducing the complexity and time required for individual configurations and increasing overall network security and efficiency.

User Account Control Settings
User Account Control (UAC) helps to prevent unauthorized changes to the system instigated by less tech-savvy users or malicious software. When

UAC is active, it limits the privileges of user accounts—even those with administrative rights. Every time a significant change is attempted, such as the installation of new software or changes to system settings, UAC prompts the user for permission or an administrator password. This ensures that users—and especially administrators—are aware of changes that could affect the system's security or stability.

By adjusting the UAC settings, administrators can set different levels of notifications and control and find a balance between security and usability. Lower settings are less intrusive but potentially less secure, while higher settings provide more prompts but increase security.

Linux Permissions

There are several methods in the Linux system to control what regular users can and cannot do:

File permissions. Defined for three categories of users: the file owner, the user group, and others. Each category can be granted or denied read, write, and execute permissions.

User groups. A fundamental aspect of Linux permissions, allowing the system administrator to assign files and directories to a group, thereby controlling which users have access to these resources.

The \<sudo\> command. Enables a regular user to perform tasks that require administrative privileges, typically reserved for the root user. This mechanism limits the scope of administrative powers, reducing the risk of accidental system-wide changes or security breaches.

By combining file permissions, user groups, and the controlled use of \<sudo\>, Linux systems effectively manage user activities and ensure that users only have the privileges necessary for their roles.

Conclusion

Limiting user admin rights is crucial to maintaining security, compliance, and control over IT systems. By restricting these rights, businesses can significantly reduce the risk of malware infections and breaches, as users with limited rights are less likely to inadvertently install malicious software or access sensitive data.

This approach also supports compliance with various regulatory standards, which often require strict control over access to sensitive information. Additionally, limiting admin rights helps in maintaining a controlled IT environment, making it easier to manage and update systems uniformly. This improves security and ensures that all users have a consistent experience with their IT resources, leading to more efficient and effective use of technology within the organization.

CHAPTER 27

Virtual Private Networks

A highly beneficial strategy for businesses is to use virtual private networks (VPNs) to provide enhanced security. They encrypt data transmitted over the internet, protecting sensitive information from hackers and cyber threats, which is especially crucial when employees are accessing the network from remote or public Wi-Fi networks.

VPNs enable the secure access of a network from remote locations. This is particularly beneficial for businesses with a mobile workforce or those who offer work-from-home options since it ensures that employees can access resources securely from anywhere. A VPN provides a secure channel for transfers, minimizing the risk of breaches and interception by unauthorized parties.

By masking the IP address and location of users, VPNs enhance privacy, keeping internet activities private and secure from competitors, especially important when researching sensitive projects or conducting market analysis. A VPN can also provide access to region-restricted resources, which is useful when needing to access content or applications that are not available in a geographic location.

As a business grows, its network needs can change. VPNs allow businesses to scale their network capabilities easily and cost effectively without extensive physical infrastructure. From a cost perspective, implementing a VPN is generally more cost effective than other security measures, especially for small to medium size businesses. It provides a high level of security without the need for significant hardware or software investments.

To effectively use VPNs, businesses should choose reliable VPN providers, ensure consistent use among employees (especially those accessing data remotely), and regularly update and maintain their VPN solutions. Combined with comprehensive training and adherence to industry-specific regulatory compliance, the result is a robust defense against cyber threats.

VPNs also optimize network performance by reducing latency and improving bandwidth efficiency, which reduces downtime and improves productivity.

What are VPNs?

VPNs come in two primary forms. Businesses should choose the type of VPN that aligns with their workforce's structure and operational needs.

Remote access. Suitable for employees working from diverse locations, say, from home offices or while traveling.

Site-to-site. Ideal for connecting the local area networks of different geographic sites, like offices in different countries, to the corporate network.

Strong security policies are a must when using VPNs. These should include details about who can access it, how authentication is managed, and the specific privileges for each user. Proper configuration of the VPN is equally vital to prevent exploitable vulnerabilities. Misconfigured VPNs are a common target for cyberattacks.

In addition to safeguarding against cyber threats, VPNs also defend against zero-day vulnerabilities, ransomware, and other malware, especially when used on company hardware that is equipped with antivirus and anti-malware software. Regular testing and monitoring of VPN capabilities are essential to ensure efficient network performance and to accommodate high user traffic.

The rise of cloud services has further emphasized the importance of VPNs, allowing businesses—especially SMBs—to securely access cloud-based applications and data storage without needing a physical data center.

Ways to Use VPNs

REMOTE WORK

It should first be noted that VPNs should only be used on company-issued devices (see Chapter 18 for insights about bring your own device situations).

Businesses should choose a VPN provider that offers robust security features, including strong encryption protocols and two-factor authentication. Reliability is key, as employees need consistent access to company resources; hence, the VPN should have a proven track record of uptime and speed.

The VPN should be user-friendly, enabling employees to connect seamlessly without requiring extensive technical knowledge. To accommodate different needs, businesses should also consider flexible VPN solutions that support a range of devices and operating systems.

Regular training and updates on VPN usage and security best practices are essential to ensure employees are aware of how to use the VPN effectively and securely. Businesses should also regularly review and update their VPN policies and infrastructure to adapt to evolving cybersecurity threats and changing work patterns.

ENCRYPTION ON PUBLIC WI-FI

Businesses should implement VPN policies for employees using unsecured public Wi-Fi to ensure data security and privacy since doing so poses significant risks like interception and hacking. A VPN encrypts internet traffic, making it difficult for cybercriminals to access sensitive information.

Businesses should mandate VPN use for any work-related activity on public networks and provide clear guidelines on accessing and using the VPN. Employee training on cybersecurity best practices, including the risks of public Wi-Fi and the importance of VPNs, is essential.

SECURE COMMUNICATION

Businesses should leverage VPNs to enhance the security of their email, file sharing, and communication processes. VPNs create an encrypted tunnel for transmission, ensuring that sensitive data remains confidential and protected from cyber threats.

For secure email communication, a VPN can prevent interception and unauthorized access, especially when employees are using public or unsecured networks. In terms of file sharing, a VPN adds a layer of security by masking IP addresses and encrypting files, safeguarding them from potential intruders or breaches. Finally, VPNs contribute to secure business communication by maintaining the privacy and integrity of voice, video, and messaging services, which is particularly vital for remote or distributed teams relying on digital communication tools.

Businesses should choose a reliable VPN provider, ensure it is consistently used by all employees, and integrate it into their overall cybersecurity strategy to maximize protection and data privacy.

INTERNATIONAL BUSINESS OPERATIONS

For businesses engaging in international operations, employing VPNs is essential. They enable secure, encrypted connections between remote employees and corporate networks, ensuring that sensitive data is accessible only to authorized personnel. This is particularly crucial in the context of the global shift towards remote work. VPNs also ensure compliance with laws like GDPR by enabling secure access to and processing of sensitive information.

In regions with internet restrictions, VPNs are particularly beneficial. They enable the bypassing of geographic restrictions, facilitating access to essential services and applications that might otherwise be inaccessible. This capability is significant for businesses operating in multiple locations, allowing teams to collaborate seamlessly using tools like Microsoft Teams and OneDrive and access internal applications securely.

SAFEGUARD CLIENT DATA

Businesses should adopt VPNs as an integral part of their security strategy, particularly in highly regulated sectors, such as law, health care, and finance in which client confidentiality is crucial. VPNs are particularly vital because they mitigate the risks associated with the kind of breaches that lead to legal repercussions, loss of client trust, and financial penalties.

RESEARCH AND DEVELOPMENT

Businesses can leverage VPNs for confidential research and development activities, ensuring that new ideas and intellectual property remain secure. By providing an encrypted connection over the Internet, they enable secure remote access to internal resources, allowing R&D teams, including those working remotely or in different geographical locations, to collaborate efficiently and access necessary data and systems securely.

In such cases, it is extremely important to choose reliable VPN services with strong encryption standards and to deeply educate R&D teams about best practices to ensure maximum security and efficiency.

MULTILOCATION BUSINESSES

Integrating VPNs into businesses that operate in multiple locations is crucial for establishing a secure and unified network. VPNs help ensure that sensitive data remains protected when transmitted across various corporate locations, significantly reducing the risk of cyber threats like hacking or breaches.

By creating a secure tunnel for transmission, VPNs ensure that employees at different locations can safely access the central network, which not only enhances data security but also promotes collaboration and consistency in business processes across different sites.

Conclusion

VPNs offer a combination of enhanced security, remote access, privacy, and cost-effectiveness, making them an essential tool for businesses in the digital age. They help safeguard sensitive information, improve network accessibility and performance, and maintain a competitive edge in the market. VPNs are a versatile and essential tool for modern businesses, enhancing flexibility and global connectivity.

Their implementation should be tailored to each business's specific needs, considering factors like the nature of the work, employee locations, and the sensitivity of the data being handled. Businesses should use VPNs primarily to enhance their cybersecurity and ensure the privacy of sensitive materials while increasing productivity and collaboration, regardless of geographic restrictions or region-specific issues.

CHAPTER 28

USB Ports Are Not a Safe Harbor

Blocking or disabling USB ports on business systems is a common security measure that organizations take for several reasons. The ubiquity of USB ports on most business computers and the difficulty in controlling their usage makes them a particularly challenging aspect of physical security. This is why a blanket policy to block access to them is often the best course of action.

No, Just No

It's just too easy to utilize USB ports to cause damage and mayhem. Here are the reasons why not letting anyone plug into them is a sound policy.

DATA LOSS PROTECTION

They can be an easy way for unauthorized individuals to extract sensitive data from a system. This is particularly important for companies dealing with confidential or proprietary information. There have been many cases where a disgruntled employee is planning on leaving the company and downloads large amounts of material to a USB thumb drive, sometimes migrating to another employer that is a competitor.

For example, if an employee says that they need to download a large PowerPoint presentation to a thumb drive to take to a client meeting, the preferred method would be to access it via a cloud environment or secure portal. Thumb drives can be lost or stolen.

MALWARE PREVENTION

Malware can be deliberately or unknowingly transferred from an infected USB device to a company's network, leading to significant security breaches. Cybercriminals have been known to leave a USB thumb drive in a parking lot, smoking area, or lobby. An employee sees it, picks it up, and wants to return it to the owner.

When they insert the thumb drive into their system to try to find the owner, they do not even have to open a file manager application for the malware to run. It does so immediately upon being inserted, infecting the host system and spreading across the network.

One of the most famous such incidents is the Stuxnet worm. Discovered in 2010, Stuxnet was a sophisticated piece of malware that targeted supervisory control and data acquisition (SCADA) systems used in industrial control systems. It was reportedly introduced to the target environment via an infected USB flash drive and led to significant damage to Iran's nuclear program.

PHYSICAL SECURITY

Open USB ports present a significant physical security threat to business systems due to their universal accessibility, ease of use, and the potential to bypass network security measures. This vulnerability can be exploited through devices like USB drives that contain harmful software.

USB ports can also be used to physically extract sensitive data from a system, circumventing traditional cybersecurity defenses. Attackers can exploit USB ports to plant hardware-based keyloggers or other spying devices, which enables the capture of confidential information like passwords and financial documents.

Conclusion

Blocking USB ports is an effective strategy. First, it greatly enhances security by preventing unauthorized data transfer. Second, it reduces the threat of malware or virus infections, as USB devices are common carriers of malicious software. Restricting their use better safeguards networks and systems from cyberattacks. Third, blocking USB ports helps maintain device integrity and prevents unauthorized use of company equipment, which is important for compliance with various regulatory standards.

Overall, this simple measure is a key aspect of a comprehensive IT security policy that defends a business's digital assets and maintains the integrity of its technology infrastructure.

CHAPTER 29

Always Be Learning

Conducting a cybersecurity assessment with an external third-party security firm is a key component of a comprehensive cybersecurity program. This has nothing to do with the quality of an internal IT or cybersecurity team or the outsourced MSSP. Even as a Chief Information Security Officer working for clients around the globe for over 20 years, I always thought it very important for me to have another set of eyes to look over the security posture of the networks I was responsible for.

Sometimes the IT and security teams are very focused on current initiatives and might inadvertently overlook a key vulnerability. Bringing in a third-party firm might identify something that was missed. On the other hand, it could confirm that you're on the right track.

Know What Just Happened…and What Might Happen

When presenting a firm's cybersecurity status to the board of directors, I like to present the results of an external cybersecurity assessment. This way it wasn't just Phil Ferraro talking about our excellent cybersecurity posture. These were very reputable external firms validating our current security system, as well as any cybersecurity initiatives we were working on. I used different firms each time, so no single one learned too much about our networks.

Conducting external third-party cybersecurity assessments is a crucial strategy for businesses to identify vulnerabilities, ensure compliance, and enhance their security posture. These are the ground rules.

REGULAR ASSESSMENTS

Businesses are increasingly advised to conduct external third-party cybersecurity assessments regularly, with the frequency often depending on the nature and size of the business (as well as the industry). Generally, it's recommended to undertake such assessments at least annually.

For businesses in highly dynamic industries, or those handling sensitive data, more frequent assessments—biannually or quarterly—may be necessary. Factors like changes in the IT environment, introduction of new technologies or compliance requirements, and a significant security incident also necessitate additional assessments.

These are crucial for identifying vulnerabilities, ensuring compliance with industry standards, and enhancing overall cybersecurity posture. Regular assessments by external experts provide a fresh perspective and can uncover issues that internal teams might overlook.

BUSINESS SIZE AND COMPLEXITY

For SMBs, an annual cybersecurity checkup is generally recommended. This frequency is usually sufficient, considering the pace at which technology and security threats evolve.

However, larger businesses or those with more complex IT infrastructures should consider more frequent assessments. Frequency for these organizations is two to four times a year, with at least one or two of these being full assessments, including data collection, questionnaires, and comprehensive reporting. This helps in continuously refining and staying on track with an action plan for addressing identified vulnerabilities and risks.

INDUSTRY REGULATIONS

Often the frequency at which businesses should conduct external third-party cybersecurity assessments depends largely on the regulations specific to their industry. Here's a summary of some of these industry-specific requirements, by sector of the economy:

1. Health care

Under the Health Insurance Portability and Accountability Act (HIPAA), health-care organizations and insurers, as well as third-party service providers, must adhere to specific cybersecurity standards to safeguard all personal health information. Although HIPAA doesn't specify the exact frequency of external assessments, its stringent data protection requirements imply a need for regular assessments.

2. Defense

Cybersecurity Maturity Model Certification (CMMC) applies to contractors providing services to the Department of Defense (DoD). These contractors must follow the Defense Federal Acquisition Regulation Supplement (DFARS) and Procedures Guidance and Information (PGI). These guidelines necessitate a comprehensive 110-point assessment, suggesting a high frequency of cybersecurity evaluations to maintain compliance.

3. Law

Law firms, often targeted for cyberattacks due to the sensitive nature of their stored materials, must make reasonable efforts to prevent data breaches. While specific frequency requirements vary by state, such as compliance with the California Consumer Privacy Act, adherence to standards like the National Institute of Standards and Technology (NIST) Cybersecurity Framework is considered best practice. It implies a need for regular cybersecurity assessments.

4. Retail

For such public-facing businesses, the Payment Card Industry Data Security Standard (PCI DSS) is crucial. This standard, maintained by major credit card companies, applies to all organizations processing card payments or holding payment card information. PCI DSS compliance requires passing a security scan, implying a regular assessment cycle, although the exact frequency is not stated.

5. General consumer data protection

In the United States, 47 states have enacted cybersecurity compliance standards requiring that organizations report security breaches involving consumer data. These regulations typically apply to any company using or storing personal identifying information (PII), indicating the need for periodic assessments to ensure compliance and safeguard against breaches.

6. Insurance

Cybersecurity regulations in the insurance sector

vary from state to state, but there's an increasing trend towards more stringent regulations. For instance, New York's Department of Financial Services proposed new cybersecurity regulations for financial organizations and insurance companies, suggesting a growing need for regular cybersecurity assessments.

7. Energy

The Federal Energy Regulatory Commission (FERC) establishes cybersecurity regulations for electric utility companies and operators that were created by the North American Electric Reliability Corporation (NERC). These critical infrastructure protection (CIP) standards imply a requirement for regular assessments to ensure compliance with these regulations.

While the exact frequency of external cybersecurity assessments can vary, depending on specific industry regulations, the overarching theme across industries is a need for regular and thorough assessments to ensure compliance and secure sensitive information.

Changing IT Infrastructure Changes Everything

Conducting an external third-party cybersecurity assessment is usually needed following significant changes to IT systems or after the implementation of new technologies. If a business undergoes substantial changes to its IT infrastructure, introduces new technology, or experiences major organizational changes, then an additional, more immediate assessment is recommended.

This proactive approach helps in promptly identifying and mitigating any potential security risks that these changes might introduce, ensuring the continuous protection of the business's digital assets. Frequent assessments, in such cases, aid in aligning the cybersecurity posture with the evolving IT environment and regulatory requirements, thereby maintaining a robust defense against emerging threats.

There are several different types and methodologies of assessments that can be conducted:

NATION-STATE ATTACK SIMULATION

This is my personal favorite. A third-party firm attacks you as if they were a state-sponsored operation, the most sophisticated cyberattackers in the world.

Often termed a "red team exercise," it simulates the tactics, techniques, and procedures (TTPs) of sophisticated nation-state attackers. It begins with extensive research and intelligence gathering to understand the business's digital infrastructure, including identifying potential vulnerabilities in software, hardware, and human elements.

The assessment team then executes planned attacks, which could range from phishing campaigns, advanced persistent threats (APTs), or the exploitation of known and unknown vulnerabilities (zero-days). Throughout the process, the team maintains stealth and sophistication, mimicking the behavior of a nation-state actor.

The goal is not just to test the existing security measures but also to assess the organization's ability to detect and respond to high-level threats. This could be the internal IT/Security team or a managed security services provider's (MSSP) security operations center (SOC) to see if it can detect and respond to the attack.

After the exercise, a detailed report is provided outlining the vulnerabilities discovered, the effectiveness of the security protocols in place, and recommendations for improvement. This report is crucial for enhancing an organization's resilience against actual nation-state cyber threats.

PHISHING CAMPAIGNS

Testing an organization's susceptibility helps to better understand employee awareness and overall preparedness against social engineering attacks. Phishing campaigns can be incorporated into the nation-state attacker simulation or conducted separately as a stand-alone. Typically, in the nation-state attacker simulation, the third-party firm would run multiple phishing campaigns over a couple of weeks.

Conducting these campaigns involves several key steps:

Design. Initially, the assessment team—usually a cy-bersecurity firm—designs simulated attacks tailored to the specific business to ensure they are realistic (though harmless). These simulations aim to test employees' awareness and response to phishing attempts, a common vector for security breaches.

Launch. The team then commences simulated attacks on the company's staff, tracking responses like click rates, information disclosure, and adherence to company protocols.

Review. After the campaign, the cybersecurity team analyzes the data to identify vulnerabilities, employee training needs, and areas where security protocols may require strengthening.

This assessment helps the business understand its susceptibility to real phishing attacks and informs strategies for improving its overall cybersecurity posture. The process is collaborative, ensuring that the company's leadership is informed and involved at every stage. The findings typically lead to targeted training programs and policy enhancements to mitigate the identified risks.

INSIDER THREAT SIMULATION
Assessing vulnerabilities to insider threats is crucial, as these can often be more damaging than

external attacks. There are two methodologies for assessing the insider threat:

1. ACTIVE TESTING

For the insider threat simulation, the third-party testing team is provided a generic company laptop and a generic (non-admin) user account. They can either connect to the network locally or remotely. Once they have network access, they attempt to escalate their account privileges to an admin level, first on the local machine and then on the network.

They will attempt to traverse the network without detection and locate sensitive material. If they do find it, they attempt to gain access to it. Next, they will attempt to quietly remove it in multiple ways—FTP, SFTP, email, secure external portals, and USB drives.

2. PASSIVE TESTING

This typically involves a multifaceted approach. The assessment begins with a thorough review of the company's existing security policies and procedures, ensuring they are adequately designed to identify and mitigate insider threats. This includes evaluating access controls, monitoring systems, and incident response plans.

The assessment team then performs a risk analysis

to identify potential vulnerabilities and threat vectors specific to insider actions. This involves analyzing employee roles and access privileges, as well as assessing the effectiveness of ongoing monitoring and anomaly detection systems. Employee awareness and training programs are also reviewed because insider threats often stem from unintentional actions by uninformed staff.

There are interviews with key personnel to understand the organizational culture and its impact on security practices. The use of advanced tools and techniques, such as data analytics and behavioral analysis, can further aid in identifying unusual patterns that might indicate malicious or negligent insider activities.

The assessment culminates in a comprehensive report detailing findings and recommendations, which includes strategies for improving policies, enhancing training programs, and implementing more effective monitoring and response mechanisms. This holistic approach ensures a robust defense against insider threats while balancing preventive measures with the ability to rapidly respond to incidents.

3. BENCHMARK ASSESSMENT

An external third-party cybersecurity benchmark

assessment is a comprehensive evaluation where an independent organization assesses a business's cybersecurity practices against established international standards like ISO27001, NIST Cybersecurity Framework (CSF), Center for Internet Security (CIS) Controls, and Payment Card Industry Data Security Standard (PCI-DSS).

This helps businesses understand their current cybersecurity posture, identify gaps in their security practices, and measure their performance against industry best practices and regulatory requirements. The process typically involves an in-depth review of the company's security policies, procedures, and technical controls.

The result is valuable insight for the business, allowing it to enhance its security measures, ensure compliance with relevant standards, and better protect against cyber threats. By benchmarking against these international standards, businesses can also demonstrate to stakeholders their commitment to cybersecurity, clients, and regulatory bodies.

The assessment can measure a company against others of the same approximate size, revenue, and industry, so the benchmarking is peer-to-peer. It's an excellent way to see what areas the company needs to focus on and where to develop prioritized initiatives for the upcoming year(s). Some of the top benchmarks include:

ISO 27001. International standard for data security management. Assessing against this standard helps establish a robust information security management system (ISMS).

NIST Cybersecurity Framework. Provides guidelines on how to prevent, detect, and respond to cyberattacks. It's a comprehensive framework widely used, especially in the United States.

CIS Controls. Developed by the Center for Internet Security, these provide a prioritized set of actions to protect organizations and data from known cyberattack vectors.

PCI DSS. The Payment Card Industry Data Security Standard applies to entities that store, process, or transmit credit card information. It aims to secure transactions against theft and fraud.

HIPAA Security Rule. Specific to the healthcare industry in the United States, this rule sets standards for safeguarding sensitive patient health information held or transferred in electronic form.

GDPR. The General Data Protection Regulation is a legal framework that sets guidelines for the collection and processing of individuals' personal information within the European Union.

Assessment Best Practices

DEFINE SCOPE EARLY

This is the primary and essential step. The scope of the assessment sets the boundaries and focus areas, ensuring that the third-party assessors and the business are aligned on what aspects of the cybersecurity posture will be evaluated. This clarity helps in identifying specific systems, networks, applications, and data that need to be examined.

A well-defined scope is vital for the effectiveness of the assessment. It guides the depth and breadth of the examination, ensuring that critical areas are not overlooked and resources are efficiently utilized. The process also typically includes a review of the company's cybersecurity policies, procedures, risk management practices, and compliance with relevant regulations.

By comprehensively understanding scope, third-party assessors can provide more accurate, relevant, and actionable insights, ultimately aiding the business in enhancing its cybersecurity resilience.

CHOOSE THE RIGHT THIRD PARTY

It's important to assess the reputation, expertise, and experience of potential vendors. This can be done by evaluating their past performance, client testimonials, and industry certifications. It's also crucial to ensure that the vendor understands the specific industry regulations and compliance standards applicable to the business.

Cost considerations are important but should not override the quality and thoroughness of the service. Additionally, the business should evaluate the methodologies and tools used by the vendor for the assessment, ensuring they are current and effective.

Communication and reporting protocols should be established to ensure transparency and effective collaboration. It is advisable to discuss and agree on how the vendor will handle any discovered vulnerabilities, including timelines for reassessment, if necessary.

This comprehensive approach helps in selecting a third party that is not only technically capable but also a good fit for the business's specific cybersecurity needs.

INVOLVE KEY STAKEHOLDERS

Stakeholders from various departments, such as IT, HR, finance, and operations, bring unique perspectives and insights. Their involvement will contribute to a more thorough understanding of the organization's cybersecurity landscape and aid in identifying specific vulnerabilities and threats relevant to different areas of the business.

Engaging stakeholders also fosters a culture of security awareness and responsibility across the organization, leading to more effective implementation of security policies and procedures. This collaborative effort also helps in prioritizing risks and allocating resources effectively, thus enhancing the overall effectiveness of the cybersecurity strategy, which ensures that the assessment aligns with business objectives and compliance requirements. Ultimately, better communication and coordination are facilitated during and after the assessment process.

PRIORITIZE REMEDIATION EFFORTS

Remediation of vulnerabilities identified in the cybersecurity assessment involves a strategic approach based on risk levels. The most critical step is to categorize vulnerabilities according to their severity, impact, and exploitability.

High-risk vulnerabilities, especially those that can lead to significant breaches or system compromises, should be addressed immediately. This prioritization is often guided by industry-standard scoring systems like the Common Vulnerability Scoring System (CVSS). Factors, such as the sensitivity of the affected systems, the data at risk, and the potential business impact, are crucial in this assessment.

It's also important to consider the resources required for remediation and the feasibility of implementing fixes in the context of business operations. Regularly scheduled reassessments should be conducted to ensure ongoing security and to address new vulnerabilities as they emerge. The goal is to create a balanced approach that mitigates the most significant risks without unnecessarily diverting resources from critical business functions.

CONTINUOUS IMPROVEMENT

After a business completes a cybersecurity assessment, it should use the results to continuously improve its cybersecurity measures. Thoroughly analyze the assessment report to identify vulnerabilities and areas needing improvement, including understanding the potential risks associated with each identified vulnerability and prioritizing them based on their severity and impact on the business.

Develop an action plan. It may involve updating software and hardware, implementing new security policies, or providing additional training to staff. Regularly updating the cybersecurity plan is crucial to incorporate defenses against new threats and trends in the cybersecurity landscape.

Continuous monitoring and regular reassessments should be conducted to ensure that the measures remain effective and to identify new vulnerabilities.

Collaboration across departments is essential to ensure that cybersecurity is integrated into all aspects of business operations.

Staying informed about the latest cybersecurity developments and adapting the security strategy accordingly is vital for maintaining robust cybersecurity measures.

CONFIDENTIALITY AND INTEGRITY

Choose a reputable and trustworthy assessment provider with a strong track record of handling sensitive data securely. Prior to the assessment, establish a clear agreement or contract specifying confidentiality terms, handling procedures, and the scope of the assessment to protect sensitive information.

Limit the assessment's access to only necessary systems and data to minimize exposure. Encrypt sensitive material and ensure that the assessment tools and methods comply with industry standards and legal requirements. Utilize secure communication channels for sharing information with the assessment team. It's also essential to maintain regular backups and to have a robust incident response plan in case of unintended breaches or system disruptions.

Conduct a thorough review of the assessment report to ensure no sensitive material has been inadvertently disclosed and implement the recommendations to enhance your cybersecurity posture.

Conclusion

Businesses should conduct external third-party cybersecurity assessments. The frequency and methodology should be tailored to their specific needs and industry requirements. Incorporating standards like ISO 27001 or the NIST framework can provide a structured approach to managing cybersecurity risks. Regular assessments, aligned with industry best practices and compliance requirements, are essential in maintaining a robust cybersecurity posture in the face of evolving threats.

Cybersecurity assessments identify and mitigate potential vulnerabilities in networks, systems, and processes. They are essential in preventing breaches and to understand and address cybersecurity risks. Regular assessments enable organizations to stay updated on ever-evolving cyber threats and to adapt their security strategies accordingly.

ABOUT THE AUTHOR

Phillip J. Ferraro is also the author of the international bestseller, *Cybersecurity: Everything an Executive Needs to Know.* He has worked globally in the cybersecurity field for over 25 years.

His most recent position was serving as a Managing Director for one of the largest financial services organizations in the world. His role was to meet with the firm's top clients around the world and help them with cybersecurity issues spanning individuals, families, and businesses.

Prior to this, Mr. Ferraro served as a Global Chief Information Security Officer (CISO) in both the public and private sectors. His responsibilities included leading worldwide information protection and enterprise cybersecurity programs and providing end-to-end planning, execution, and delivery of secure global computing architecture infrastructure, with a focus on cybersecurity, protection, and data egress prevention.

Mr. Ferraro has been an advisor to C-suite executives and board-level directors. He has provided extensive and demonstrated knowledge of cybersecurity risk management, developed and implemented world-class cybersecurity programs, and ensured compliance with multiple regulatory standards.

His extensive cyber background and experience include CISO roles with the US Department of Defense, the Intelligence Community at large, and two large Fortune 500 firms for which he developed and implemented strategic, comprehensive global enterprise cybersecurity and risk management programs.

He is an accomplished author and sought-after international keynote speaker on cybersecurity and is recognized as one of the top CISOs in the country. He is also among the few who have presented testimony about advanced cyber threats to both Senate and Congressional committees on Capitol Hill.

Mr. Ferraro became a subject matter expert in cyber espionage while serving in the US federal government for 30 years, including positions where he was instrumental in revitalizing cybersecurity programs and significantly increasing the overall security posture.

Additionally, he served in the US Army Special Forces (Green Berets), including numerous overseas tours and combat operations in Southeast Asia, Central and South America, and the Middle East.

Mr. Ferraro holds a Master's in Information Technology and a Bachelor's in Business Administration. His numerous information security and technology industry certifications include:

- Certified Information Systems Security Professional (CISSP)

- Certified Information Security Manager (CISM)
- Certified Ethical Hacker (CEH)
- Cisco Certified Network Engineer (CCNE)
- Checkpoint Certified Security Engineer (CCSE)
- Microsoft Certified Security Engineer (MCSE)

www.phillipferraro.com.